Jesus I Know...but

Who Are You?

Discovering Your True Authority in Christ

PUBLISHED BY: Leta Patrick

Copyright © 2025 by Leta M. Patrick
All rights reserved. No part of this book may be copied, stored, or transmitted in any form without the written permission of the author, except for brief quotations used in reviews or articles.

Scripture Citations
Scripture quotations in this book are taken from the King James Version (KJV) and Young's Literal Translation (YLT) of the Bible.

Published by Leta Patrick
ISBN: 979-8-9925912-1-7

This book is a work of non-fiction. While every effort has been made to ensure accuracy, the author assumes no responsibility for errors or omissions. The reader is encouraged to study the Bible and seek God's guidance in all matters.

First Printing: February 2025

Acknowledgment

Words cannot fully capture how thankful I am for God being my Lord and Savior. First and foremost, I thank Him for showing me who I am in Him and for placing this book on my heart. Every word written is because of His grace, wisdom, and guidance.

Mark, you are the piece of my life I never realized was missing. God may not have made a perfect man other than Jesus, but He made the perfect one for me when He made you. Your smile is the first thing I look forward to every morning, and your unwavering support strengthens me in every way. You are my safe place, my steady hand, and the one who helps keep me anchored in the storms of life.

The Lord knew just what I needed when He blessed me with my baby girl. From the very beginning, she brought a light into my life that I did not even realize I needed. Alina has been my sounding board through all the highs and lows for as long as I can remember, and as a young woman, she still is. But over the years, our conversations have shifted. What once was me pouring into her has turned into us pouring into each other, sharing, and discussing God daily. Watching her grow in Him has been one of the greatest blessings of my life.

Cainan, mama's little *Promise Land*. I prayed for you, and God answered. You came into this world wired and full of life, always keeping me on my toes. You have challenged me in ways I never expected, but in the best way possible. You help to bring out a **fight for life** in me in a way I cannot explain, and I would not trade it for anything. I also see the spiritual growth in you, and I know God is giving the increase.

Amber and Twain, though you were not raised in my home, you have always been a part of my heart and my love for you has never changed. Amber, I trust in God's hand over your life, and I believe in the vision He has for you. His purpose for you is just as strong as ever. Twain, seeing God move in your life has been such a blessing. I look forward to all He has in store for you and your family, knowing His plans are greater than we can imagine and His work in you is only just beginning.

Growing up, Mama's faith and love built the foundation of our home. Her wisdom still guides me, and I am forever grateful for the life she lived. She taught my sister and me to seek God in everything—and my sister took that at face value, always trying to step in as Mama #2 whenever she could! For my sister's heart of gold and advice, I will always be thankful. I carry Mama's faith, wisdom, and kindness with me every single day.

Before I go any further, I want to thank you for taking the time to read my book. My name is Leta (sounds like Leeta) M. Patrick, but you can call me Lee! I was named after both of my grandmothers, Leta Marie, and I carry that name with honor.

Dedication

"Grandma, I don't want to hear that." Those were often my thoughts—not so much when she tried to teach me about the Bible, but when she corrected others. She had a boldness about herself, one that sometimes made me uncomfortable as a young girl who genuinely loved people and wanted to keep the peace. I did not like what I perceived as negativity, but what I did not understand at the time was that she was not being negative at all. She was teaching truth—uncompromising, unwavering truth.

To truly understand the Word of God, one must have a heart that seeks the truth, be filled with the Holy Spirit, and possess a willingness to renew their mind. Without a sincere desire for truth, a person will only see what they want to see or what they have been taught to see. True understanding comes when you are willing to lay aside preconceived notions and let God reveal His truth through His Word (**John 16:13**).

The Bible is spiritually discerned (**1 Corinthians 2:14**). Without the Holy Spirit, a person may read the Word but miss the deeper revelation. Jesus said the Holy Spirit would teach us all things (**John 14:26**), meaning you must rely on His leading, not just human reasoning.

Rightly Dividing the Word: Understanding Context

To fully grasp the teachings in this book, it is imperative to recognize the reading of Scripture in its proper context. Many misunderstandings arise when verses are read in isolation rather than as part of the broader passage in which they were written.

A prime example of this is **John 12:32**:

"And I, if I be lifted up from the earth, will draw all (men) unto me."

Some believe this verse means that if you praise God, He will draw all people to Himself. However, this misunderstanding comes from not recognizing both the original language and the context in which Jesus was speaking.

In the King James Bible, *italicized* words indicate they were not in the original Greek or Hebrew scriptures. When King James commissioned theologians to translate the Bible into English, they added words they **believed** would make the text read more smoothly. While their intention was clarity, this sometimes altered the meaning.

King James went even further in making changes—he had the book of Jacob renamed to James, simply because he wanted his name in the Bible. While this change does not affect doctrine, it is important to recognize how translation decisions like this have shaped what you read today.

If you read **John 12:32** in its full context, you will see that the surrounding subject is judgment—not worship or praise. The verse itself states: *"And I, if I be lifted up (on the cross), will draw all (judgment) unto me."*

Jesus was not saying that if people praised Him, others would be drawn to Him. Instead, He was declaring that when He was crucified, all judgment would be placed upon Him.

In essence, He was saying (paraphrasing):

When He went to the cross, mankind would no longer be judged based on their actions. He did not come to condemn the world for what they do or do not do, but *"that the world through him might be saved"* (**John 3:17**).

Jesus took the judgment upon Himself because mankind had failed to keep the Law (**Romans 3:23**). The issue was not with the Law itself, but with humanity's inability to uphold it (**Hebrews 8:7-8**). That is why Jesus established a New Covenant—one in which He bore the full penalty for sin and secured eternal redemption through His sacrifice, covering all sins—past, present, and future (**Hebrews 9:12, 26**). By studying Scripture with discernment, you see that Jesus was not talking about praise—He was talking about taking the full weight of judgment upon Himself at the cross.

For reference, I primarily use the King James Version (KJV) when writing this book. However, unless otherwise noted, I will also refer to Young's Literal Translation (YLT), as it often aligns more closely with how the scriptures were originally written.

A Legacy of Biblical Truth

I once heard a saying: *'Many people won't let the Bible get in the way of what they believe to be true.'* Over the years, I have seen just how true this is. They hold tightly to long-held beliefs, personal interpretation, or teachings passed down to them, but they never take the time to truly study the Word for themselves—to seek understanding beyond what they have been told and allow Scripture to shape their beliefs rather than the other way around.

My grandma Leta was different. She did not always follow traditions or conform to what was commonly accepted. She had a deep understanding of the Bible and was unafraid to share it, even if it meant stepping on toes. What I now realize is that she was teaching me to rightly divide the Word—not through the lens of religious customs, but according to the New Covenant of Grace. She had a way of cutting through the noise and going straight to the heart of Scripture, showing me how to separate the shadow of the Old Testament from the fulfillment found in the New Testament.

While my mama was instrumental in teaching me about Jesus, serving others, and distinguishing right from wrong, it was my grandma Leta who laid the foundation for my understanding of biblical principles. She was my Paul. As Paul wrote in **1 Corinthians 3:6:**

"I have planted; Apollos watered; but God gave the increase."

Grandma Leta, like Paul, was bold, unafraid to tell the truth, and unwavering in her faith. She was key in planting seeds of truth in my life.

I write this book in remembrance of her, Leta Patrick Jacobs—for the wisdom she shared, the truths she imparted, and the legacy she left. It is because of her that I have come to understand the power and beauty of the New Covenant of Grace. Her teachings helped me see that the Old Testament was a shadow of things to come and that, through Jesus Christ, you now live under grace.

As I share these truths in this book, I pray they plant seeds in your heart as well, just as she did in mine. I hope they challenge you, encourage you, and inspire you to seek not just knowledge of the Word, but a clear and Spirit-led understanding of it.

Throughout this journey, I also want to acknowledge the countless teachers, preachers, and mentors whose insights have helped to shape my understanding of the Word. While I may not mention each one by name, their influence has been significant. I am grateful for the seeds they have sown and for the ways they have deepened my knowledge and faith.

I dedicate this work to grandma, and I thank God for placing her in my life to guide me in truth. The following excerpt, handwritten in my Bible on June 30, 2023, was the moment God first laid this book on my heart. I had been writing for years but never fully understood the depth of what God was revealing—or the depth of what He was calling me to do—until that moment. It all began with a simple revelation—moving from performance to believing. Grandma Leta's teachings planted the seeds, and this book is the fruit of that journey.

> 2 Tim:
> Rightly Dividing the Word is Key!
> Seeds from Grandma Lita's teaching!
> 6-30-23 - The entire New Testament is not on doing but BELIEVING!!!
> The Old Testament was performance based according to Mosaic Law - I do, then God does.
> New Testament - Acts - Rev, is Believing Jesus already did it when He said "It is Finished"
> It's no longer performance based but believing.
> Matthew, Mark, Luke, John - Jesus was fulfilling 2-fold ministry - He was living still under the law and keeping the law according to prophecy (He was the only one who could) and yet He was preparing the way so that when He died and rose again we would no longer be under the law but under grace.

Yes, I know my handwriting looks like I wrote this while riding a rollercoaster—but thankfully, God reads the heart, not the penmanship.

Introduction: Jesus I Know...but Who Are You?

It is a question every believer must face: Do you truly know the power that resides within you? Believers today struggle to resist the enemy, overcome temptation, or walk in victory—not because they lack salvation, but because they lack the revelation of their authority in Christ.

This book is an opportunity to discover and embrace the authority given to us by God through Jesus Christ and the indwelling Holy Spirit. It is not just about what you believe; it is about **knowing** who you are and the divine power at work within you. When the Holy Spirit resides in you, Satan recognizes it. He knows the authority you carry—*but do you*?

In **Acts 19:15**, an evil spirit confronted a group of men attempting to cast it out: *"Jesus I know, and Paul I know; but who are you?"* The spirit knew Jesus and acknowledged Paul because Paul operated in his God-given authority. But the sons of Sceva had only heard of Jesus and attempted to use His name without a personal relationship with Him. They treated His name as a tool, lacking the faith and connection required to operate in its power. As a result, they were overpowered.

Many Christians today face similar challenges. They acknowledge Jesus with their lips but do not walk in the fullness of His authority. They pray timid prayers, beg for what God has already provided, and live as though the enemy has more power than the Holy Spirit within them.

A Dream of Authority

The Holy Spirit gave me a vivid revelation of this truth through a dream. I was sitting across from a woman possessed by a demonic spirit. Immediately, I could see into the spiritual realm and recognize Satan's presence on her. As I rebuked him, the power of the Holy Spirit within me became so strong that I began to ascend toward the ceiling. The authority in me was undeniable, even to Satan himself.

I declared, *"I need to lay hands on her."* The moment I descended and stepped toward her, Satan instantly backed up—not because of my strength, but because of the Holy Spirit's power. He recognized Christ within me. When I woke up, the Holy Spirit spoke clearly:

"Many cannot cast the devil out because they don't know Me, the authority they have within."

This book will walk you through that revelation. We will explore the biblical foundation for authority, how it was lost through sin and restored through Jesus, and how we, as believers, can step into our rightful position. It is time to stop living as though you are powerless. It is time to boldly declare, act in faith, and make the enemy tremble because of the authority of Christ in you.

Living Under Grace, Not the Law

The ability to rightly divide the Word of Truth between the Old and New Testament hinges on one profound realization: <u>you are no longer under the law</u>. For clarification, it does not mean we do not keep the law but simply that we are not justified by it. Our righteousness comes through faith in Jesus, not by our ability to uphold the law. Instead of striving to measure up, we now live from a place of grace—where obedience flows from relationship, not obligation. Yet some approach Scripture as if they must still *earn* God's favor or intervention through works. Just as in Jesus' day, they *still* struggle to let go of tradition and legalism, often without realizing how it affects their faith and the faith of others.

This mindset keeps believers striving, performing, and hoping to be *'good enough'* for God's help. But **Romans 6:14** declared:

"For sin shall not have dominion over you: for <u>ye</u> <u>are</u> <u>not</u> <u>under</u> <u>the</u> <u>law</u>, but under grace."

Until you grasp this truth and stop approaching God as if <u>He is</u> holding back, you will continue to read Scripture through the lens of works-based righteousness. But Christ has done the work.

"Beware of the Leaven"

Matthew 16:1-12 reflects **Jesus' warning** about how even a small influence of tradition, legalism, or misunderstanding can shape the way we see God and live out our faith. Man-made traditions—along with interpretations passed down for generations—can strip His Word of its authority. *"Making the word of God of none effect through your tradition, which ye have delivered: and many such like things do ye."* (**Mark 7:13**). This discussion will stand strong on its own, exposing the dangers of modern-day Pharisee-like mindsets while pointing people toward true grace.

Judging the Pharisees: A Lesson in Truth and Love

It is easy to read the scriptures about the scribes and Pharisees and view them as the ones who opposed Jesus, clung to traditions, and rejected the truth standing right in front of them. But if you are not careful, you too, can fall into the same trap—valuing religious traditions over a genuine relationship with God. Rather than seeing them only as an example of what *they* did wrong, we can recognize the warning for *ourselves*. Jesus' words to them serve as a reminder to examine our own hearts, ensuring that we do not allow pride or tradition to keep us from fully embracing the truth.

Jesus rebuked the Pharisees not because He hated them, but because **He loved them enough to tell them the truth.** He exposed their hypocrisy, their legalism, and their spiritual blindness—not as an act of condemnation, but as an invitation to repent. Even in their stubbornness, He never dismissed them as hopeless. Some of them, like Nicodemus, eventually came to faith. Others might have had hardened hearts, but Christ still died for them, just as He died for every sinner.

The danger for us today is that in exposing well-meaning but false teachings, it can be easy to fall into judgmentalism—assuming we know the motives and hearts of others. Jesus never did this. He pointed out what was wrong—clearly and boldly—but He never demeaned or belittled anyone. He corrected, but He also extended grace.

There is a fine line between calling out falsehood and sitting in self-righteous judgment. The moment you begin looking down on others as if you yourself are incapable of being deceived, you are walking in the same pride that blinded the Pharisees. Here is the unshakable reality: anyone can become a Pharisee. Legalism can creep into any church, any teaching, and any heart. The moment you begin valuing traditions over truth, performance over relationship, and appearance over authenticity, you are falling into the same traps that Jesus warned about.

All my life, I thought persecution would come from the secular world, but that was not so. Some of the strongest opposition you will ever face will probably come from well-meaning believers who sincerely believe they are defending their faith—and I get it, because that well-meaning believer was me. And here is the reality—people take offense when their beliefs are challenged. There will be those who will resist. Some will argue. Others will label it heresy, even when it is simply the truth of God's Word. Persecution will come because traditions are comfortable, and truth disrupts that comfort. Jesus Himself faced this resistance at every turn, not from the sinners and outcasts, but from the religious leaders—the very people who thought they were closest to God.

So, as you walk in truth, the Bible instructs to do so with both boldness and humility. Boldness to stand firm on God's Word, to expose Satan's deception, and to call people into freedom. But also, humility—because *we, too, have been shown grace.* Every one of us is on a journey of learning, unlearning, and growing in the knowledge of Christ.

When the time comes and opposition arises, remember *we are not here to win arguments.* You are here to set people free. Jesus did not come to shame people into repentance—He came to lead them to the truth through love. And that is how we are to walk.

Final Thoughts

Many of believers spend years feeling like there is always *more* they need to do—more striving, more performing, more proving themselves worthy of God's blessings. But you can be sure of this, Christ has done the work. As Paul explains in **Romans 7:4-6** and **Galatians 3:24-25**, the law served its purpose, but now you are called to live by faith under grace and believe it.

This book is about **resting** in Him. Maybe you have felt like you are constantly reaching but never quite grasping the promises of God. But what if the struggle was not necessary? What if you have been equipped all along?

Table of Contents

Section 1: The Foundation of Authority

1. Dominion (Authority) Lost and Restored
2. Shaped in the Shadows
3. Breaking Through Unbelief

Section 2: Authority and Spiritual Warfare

4. The Power Switch
5. Satan's Tug of War: Pulled by Doubt, Pushed by Pride
6. Behind Enemy Lines: The War Unseen - Discernment
7. Winning the War: Before It Begins
8. 'I' Planted

Section 3: Healing and the New Covenant

9. Taking Charge: Authority Over Sickness and Healing
10. Sin, Sickness, and The Cross
11. 'Already'

Section 4: Walking in Truth and Transformation

12. Restoring Faith-Based Prayer

13. Stop Chasing a Dollar

14. Replacing Lies

15. Attacking the Root, Not the Fruit

Section 5: Grace and the New Covenant

16. The Transformative Power of Grace

17. Hell? No!

18. Neither Do I Condemn Thee

19. Staying Rooted in Grace

20. What If God Really Forgot?

21. Anointed, Not Appointed

22. The Law Is Not Destroyed

Section 6: Spiritual Maturity and Worship

23. The Other Side of Submission

24. Clean Heart, Not Just a Clean Cup

25. Worship Beyond the Walls

26. Out of the Shadows, Into His Rest

27. The Unshakeable Promise of Grace

Section 7: The Journey Continues

28. Dying to 'I': A Vision to See

29. The Most Intimate Relationship

30. How It All Ties Together

31. Be Still and Know That I Am God

Thank You

Dominion (Authority) Lost and Restored

Have you ever experienced something so traumatic that it completely turned your life around in a matter of seconds—so unexpected that it left you reeling?

Nothing could have prepared me for what happened the day my mother had a stroke. One moment, life felt normal—routine, even. The next, we were thrown into a whirlwind of trauma, confusion, and fear. No one paused to explain what was happening, what decisions we would soon face, or just how drastically life was about to change— because there was not time. We were left to figure it out, one overwhelming moment after another.

That sinking feeling of helplessness and frustration is a faint echo of what humanity experienced after the fall in the Garden of Eden. One moment, Adam and Eve walked in perfect fellowship with God, entrusted with the position of rulership over creation. The next, everything shifted. Sin slammed the door to the life they had known, stripping them of the authority they were designed to carry. Suddenly, humanity was no longer walking in confidence but struggling under the weight of a world they were never intended to serve.

But here is the difference: when this happened to Mama, our ability to stand in authority was not gone. It was in us, even if we had not fully realized it yet.

The fullness of what had been given was there, but stepping into it was a process—just as it is for many believers today. And that is why this is so important. Throughout this book, each truth revealed is meant to help you **recognize what is already inside you.**

When the Enemy Strikes!

I had been trying to close out my book for weeks, but every time I thought I was done, God would reveal something else that needed to go in. Then, the week I was supposed to publish, something happened.

Immediately, I felt that same despair—the one that had crept through my life for years. The same despair that kept me bound as a child and well into adulthood. I had just finished adding the next section, ran some errands, and on my way home, Satan tried to plant thoughts of defeat, agony, heaviness—you name it. But the crazy thing? I had just written about recognizing these attacks when they come!

Mind you, I was *dead* to this stuff. (*Explained in more detail in Chapter 23: The Other Side of Submission.*) I had died to all the nonsense I once allowed Satan to use against me. Yet here it was, not just staring at me in the face, but trying to take the very breath out of me.

I came home, recognized it for what it was, and prayed. But my mind kept drifting back to it. So, I left the house and walked to where my husband was working in our building. He was so greased up, under the truck, fighting the motor, and then had me jacking the truck up—I didn't even have time to be in my feelings (which is exactly what was happening).

I walked back in, texted my daughter, and said, *"Sissy, are you gone to bed?"* She said, *"Yes, goodnight, Mama."* I said, *"Goodnight."* And right then, I *knew* God was stirring me away from venting.

I got in the shower, but the thoughts kept creeping in. Finally, I said, *STOP!* I started speaking in tongues and commanded that mess to leave *right then*. And that's when God spoke to my spirit: *"Did I not give you revelation about laughing in the face of the enemy?"*

I chuckled a little, stepped out of that shower, and started praising God—thanking Him for reminding me that I had secured victory. The same thing I once saw as *life or death*—yes, I was once *that* dramatic in my feelings—was nothing but a weak attempt from the enemy.

God had made it clear that as I wrote this book, I would encounter resistance in ways I could not predict. At some point, you may also face resistance—whether from friends, family, or even those who barely know you. Some will only recognize God's work in your life when they see the physical fruit because they do not understand what He is doing at the root. And that is okay—because it is not their place to. So, stop focusing on Satan's distractions!

Listen, let me explain something to you: People will misunderstand you. They will question your motives, dismiss what you carry, attack your character, and even make you feel like what you are doing does not matter. And if you are not careful, you will start striving for validation—trying to prove yourself to people who were never meant to see what God placed in you.

It is not being *hateful*—as we call it—but do you really *care?* Because if your focus is on gaining approval, if you are constantly weighed down by what people think or how they treat you, then you are walking in the flesh—just like I was about to be, again.

Now, I am not telling you to pick up your Bible and read it hourly or even daily—that is not my place. But *that desire* **will** *come.* I am encouraging you to seek God first, and as you do, everything you need will be added to you *as* through His Word.

You might be thinking, *"I read my Bible, but I still don't get it."* Let this sink in, it is not that the answers are not there—it is that you have been looking through the wrong lens. Your perception determines **what** you receive, and if you have been conditioned by tradition or legalism, you can overlook the truth even when it is right in front of you.

Did you know that *creation itself* is waiting for the sons and daughters of God to *get* the truth of His Word? **Romans 8:19** *says, "For the earnest expectation of the creation eagerly waits for the revealing of the sons of God."* When you step into rightly dividing the *shadow* of the Old Testament from the *revelation* of what the New Testament of Grace has to offer, you **shatter** the gates of hell that have reigned over your life for so long—*wide, slap open!*

That is what hell fears.

Hell does not fear you being saved. It does not care if you are the best person on earth—serving, supporting others, and helping all who are in need. The enemy does not mind you staying busy with good works—his goal is to keep you unaware of your identity in Christ.

That following morning, I woke to laughter—my own. At some point, my daughter had even texted back, *"Mama, is everything okay?"* But that was **God's way** of shutting down the pity party I was about to throw. Is that not just like Him? He did not let anyone RSVP to my meltdown. It all stayed *between me and Him* because, as He took out the trash, I went to bed and slept like an infant—*all night long.*

That is **resting in Christ.**

I Am a Threat

My son called me after one of his college basketball games and said, *"Mama, I went back and watched my high school videos—how I made most of my shots—and I realized something: I'm a threat."*

He was not bragging. As a freshman in college, he has spent a lot of time on the bench—a big shift from being a key scorer in high school. He has been learning to adjust, to fight through the challenge of feeling like he is starting over.

The moment he said it; I could not contain myself. *"Son, that's it!"* I shouted.

Then he added, *"Mama, I got my smile back."*

That is the thing about feeling defeated—it steals every bit of your joy. But when your confidence returns? *Watch out!*

It does not matter what life tries to dictate to you—what matters is how you see yourself, and more importantly, how God sees you. *You are a threat to Satan's plans.* Once you grasp that revelation, there is no going back. You step into the reality of who you truly are.

I **know** I am a threat to Satan, and he knows it too. *And so are you.*

That is the revelation every believer needs to walk in true authority. That is why I could wake up laughing that morning. God had already shown me the power of laughing in the face of opposition long before I finished this book. But here is the key: **without revelation, laughter alone will not break the bondage. Without immersing yourself in the Word, you will not receive the revelation.**

And revelation changes everything.

With that, let me tell you what God gave me several nights ago. It was simple. It was clear. And it is something you need to hear...
STOP.

I do not care how bad it is or how stuck you may feel.

STOP.

Right now.
Shut <u>everything</u> else out.

The Holy Ghost woke me up from a dead sleep to tell you this—this is your **wake-up call.**

Do you think you are trapped, with no way out?
Do you think this is just your life now and the outcome to it lies in someone else's hands?
Do you think every time you are on the edge of breakthrough something else happens?

That…is a LIE.

And I need you to hear this with everything in you—**Satan is banking on you never realizing the truth.**

He does not have to steal your faith.
He just has to keep you blind.

Blind to who you are.
Blind to the authority you have.
Blind to the fact that he has already been defeated.

The enemy constantly feeds your thoughts like:

"This is how it just is."
"You'll never get out of this."

"You're too tired to fight."
"Nothing ever changes."
"Look how long you've been going through this."

And you have bought it.

You are walking around **carrying chains that are not even locked.** You have unknowingly allowed the enemy to plant strongholds in your thinking, shaping how you see your future.

But hear me—it is one of the biggest lies **to ever come from the pits of hell.**

Jesus did not **almost** win.
He did not **partially** break the chains.

IT. IS. FINISHED.

That means Satan has **NO authority** over you—**unless** you hand it to him.

You are exhausted **because** you have been fighting wrong.

You are tired **because** you have been trying to win a battle that has already been won.

You feel hopeless **because** you have been waiting for something to change instead of standing in what Christ finished at the Cross.

In simple terms, you have been **too blind** to see the way out because you have been wearing glasses **Satan prescribed**.

And to top it off—you have been swinging at demons that were **already knocked out at the cross!**

Read that again.

They were already defeated.

But Satan does not need you to believe that. He just needs you to keep your head down—worn out, beaten down, and convinced that this is just how life is.

Again…**Lies.**

This is where it stops.

Not next week.
Not when the bills go away.
Not when the people in your life change.

RIGHT NOW.

You will understand more **how to stand** in the authority you have as you continue through this book, but—

Stand up.
Open your mouth.
And you start **PRAISING HIM.**

Because this is the **moment** your breakthrough begins.

When you praise in the fire, you remind hell to whom you belong.

You are **not weak.** You are **not helpless.** And you are certainly **not stuck.** You are a **blood-bought, grace-covered, Spirit-empowered child of God.** So, **hold your head up and walk like it.**

Satan is not your master.
Circumstances are not your prison.
Ephesians 2:6 tells you; you have been positioned with Christ:

*"And God <u>raised</u> us up with Christ and <u>**seated**</u> **us with Him** in the heavenly realms in Christ Jesus."*

The moment you saw it and gave God the glory, the chains fell off.

Because **YOU. ARE. FREE.**

You just broke through.

Sin Has No Hold on You

Living in this truth means understanding that sin no longer has authority over us. **Romans 6:14** boldly declares, *"Sin shall not have dominion over you, for you are <u>not under law but under grace</u>."*

Let that sink in for a moment. Ask yourself: **What does that truly mean?** We will explore this further in the chapters ahead, but for now, hold onto that question as you continue reading.

This freedom is not a license to live recklessly—it is an empowerment to live righteously, knowing our place before God is secure. This truth has depth, and it is worth pausing to reflect on its significance.

Victory Over the Enemy

Satan thrives on false accusations. He wants believers to remain blind of who they are in Christ because **a believer who does not know their authority will not exercise it.** But the moment you grasp your identity; the enemy's schemes collapse.

Colossians 1:13 affirms this truth: *"[God] has delivered us from the dominion of darkness and transferred us into the kingdom of His beloved Son."*

Notice the wording—*delivered* and *transferred*. This is not a future promise; it is a <u>present reality</u>. You are no longer under the rule of darkness. You have been repositioned into God's kingdom, with full rights and access.

As you move forward chapter by chapter, you will begin to see more clearly how Satan has used subtle deception to mislead many. There are countless God-fearing, God-seeking individuals—perhaps even you—whose hearts are undoubtedly in the right place, yet whose minds have been unknowingly shaped by lies from the enemy disguised as truth.

Living as Sons and Daughters

The final piece of this restored power is our identity. Under the Old Covenant, access to God required rituals, sacrifices, and strict adherence to laws. But under the New Covenant, you come as sons and daughters.

Galatians 4:6 says, *"Because you are sons, God has sent forth the Spirit of His Son into your hearts, crying out, 'Abba, Father!'"*

This changes everything. You no longer approach God from a place of fear or performance. You come boldly as His children, fully accepted, fully equipped, and fully empowered.

Stepping Into What is Already Yours

Restored dominion is not just a concept—it is the reality God intended for you to walk in. You are not waiting for more power, more authority, or some future breakthrough. **Everything you need has already been secured through Christ.** Now, it is time to let go of striving, silence the lies of the enemy, and step fully into the truth of who you are. **When you embrace this, your life will no longer reflect struggle—it will reflect victory.**

Shaped in the Shadows

Your Story is Just Beginning

Throughout the Bible, you see God preparing His people for great tasks, often through seasons of trials, periods of waiting, and growth. Abraham did not just wake up one day ready to sacrifice Isaac—the son God had promised him. That *level of faith* came through years of trusting God through the unknown. Joseph did not allow anger or resentment to take root as he endured betrayal, slavery, and imprisonment; instead, he chose to trust God's plan. David faced monumental obstacles—not just for himself, but for an entire nation— yet he ran **toward** Goliath with unshakable faith. Elijah and Jeremiah endured isolation, rejection, and hardship, but their challenges strengthened their trust in God's provision. And then there's Moses: a man marked by past mistakes, including murder, and a long season in the wilderness. Each of these examples proves a powerful truth: God shapes His people in the hidden places, long before their purpose is revealed to the world.

But growth does not happen overnight. Faith, wisdom, and maturity are built over time—not just in the lives of biblical heroes but in our own as well.

Just like faith is built over time, so is understanding. Maturity takes time, and as children, we often do not grasp the full weight of life or even the words spoken to us. My father would tell my sister and me, *"You just don't understand, you're too young to know— but one day you will."* He said it so many times I could not count, and

I remember my sister looking up and saying, *"Well, what good is that doing us now?"* Then we would laugh. At the time, it felt like an answer that left us in the dark, as if understanding were always just out of reach.

But now, I see the truth in his words. As a child, I thought as a child, reasoned as a child. Yet, as I grew, the wisdom that once seemed distant became clear. And just as our father's words lingered in our hearts, **the Word of the Lord never departs**. Understanding may not come all at once, but when we walk with Him, it grows within us, *shaping* our perspective.

The Wilderness Is Preparation, Not Punishment

Moses' forty years in the wilderness may have seemed like running from past mistakes, but it was a season of preparation. He could have been shaped in the palace, yet God met him where he was and still used him.

For decades, Moses tended sheep—far from the life he once knew. He may have wondered if he had ruined his purpose, but God had other plans. Those years were not wasted; they refined him. In solitude, he learned patience and humility. Leading stubborn flocks prepared him to lead a nation through the wilderness for another forty years.

What seems like a delay in your life might be your greatest season of equipping. God wastes nothing—every struggle, mistake, and moment of waiting is shaping you for what He has called you to do.

He's STILL Writing Your Chapter

The enemy wants you, as a believer, to think it is over. That this pain in life is all there is and all there will ever be. God is not just getting you through this—He is preparing you. The same

God who called Moses from the wilderness, who turned Joseph's pit into a palace, and who brought David from the pasture to the throne—that same God is working in your life, too. You may see it to some degree or not at all *right now*, but He **is** shaping you for a purpose beyond what you can imagine. Hold on. This is not the end.

Equipped

You see, I knew God—or at least, I thought I did. I read the Word, but I did not yet know how to divide it rightly. I went through years of struggle, asking why certain things kept happening. Why did I feel so powerless when I knew the promises of God?

It was not until much later that I realized the issue was not just what I faced—it was how unprepared I was to face it.

Life is unpredictable. One wrong move, one careless miscalculation, and everything can come crashing down. It reminds me of a job I have done countless times with my husband—a job that demands precision, wisdom, and preparation: *tree removal.*

Imagine this: My husband, a welder by trade with decades of experience, is also highly skilled in rigging—the art of using ropes, chains, and pulleys to lift and secure heavy objects. It is not about brute strength; it is about strategy, balance, and control. Picture him in a bucket, 60 to 70 feet in the air, cutting massive limbs from towering trees, while I work below, clearing debris and keeping everything moving.

Here is the thing—one wrong cut, one unsecured limb, and disaster is inevitable. If he miscalculates the weight or fails to secure a branch properly, it does not just fall—it swings, crashes, and destroys everything in its path. And guess who is standing below? That's right—me, positioned as the unintentional crash-test dummy.

The same is true with the Word of God. It is not just something to skim through casually; it is a lifesaving, enemy-defeating weapon. Just as my husband must master weight distribution, angles, and rigging techniques to prevent disaster, you must learn to rightly divide the Word to navigate life's spiritual battles.

Without proper knowledge and skill, a person is reckless. They move without wisdom, react without strategy, and set themselves up for failure. But when you are trained in the Word, when you apply it with precision, Satan has far less room to strike—much less prevail.

Breaking Free

If you are facing struggles—whether it is financial burdens, broken relationships, health challenges, addictions, or even the worry of your children being lost in this world—it doesn't matter what it is. I do not say that lightly.

While God is sovereign, He is not sitting in heaven with a computer mouse, clicking through your life and controlling every detail like:

"Yes, you've prayed enough today."
"Yes, you've attended enough services."
"Yes, you've pleaded and served enough, so I'll remove this thorn now."

That is **not** how He operates.

Under Grace, He has empowered you to rise above whatever you are facing. But people suffer because they live in ignorance of the Word. I do not say this to hurt you; I say it to wake you up and open your eyes to the power that already lives within you.

Rock Bottom to Restoration

I know because I was probably the most ignorant of them all. And because of that, I became one of the most desperate. I did not just hit rock bottom—I slammed into it, hard. I was so low that I prayed one of the most desperate, misguided prayers a person could pray: I asked God to take my life and deliver me through death.

That prayer was not born out of faith—it was the result of years of poor choices and a desperate search for freedom.

But here is the beautiful thing about God:
He did not leave me there.

Your Freedom Starts Here

No matter how heavy the burden is or how impossible the situation feels, freedom is not a distant hope—it is a reality that has been secured.

Everything you thought was lost? He has redeemed it.

Every wound that felt too deep? He has healed it.

Every battle you have been fighting alone? He has won it.

What if the very thing meant to break you is the thing God can use to restore you?

Restoration is not something to strive for—it is already taking place. What was lost has been reclaimed, what was broken is being rebuilt, and what once seemed impossible is becoming a testimony of His power.

But here is the real question—do you believe it? Do you truly believe that freedom is yours, that healing has already been provided, that restoration is not just possible but already in motion? Because the greatest battle is **not** in your circumstances—it is in your mind. The enemy's greatest weapon is not power, but deception, and his most dangerous lie is that you still have to *earn* what has already been given.

That is where unbelief takes root. And that is where it must be confronted.

Breaking Through Unbelief

Unbelief is a struggle as old as humanity itself. It is woven throughout both the Old and New Testaments, and if I am honest, it is something I have wrestled with personally. Trusting God's promises, even when they are clearly stated in His Word, does not always come naturally. My journey from doubt to bold faith has been one of learning, growing, and discovering the transformative power of truly understanding and rightly dividing the Word of Truth.

Unbelief is not just a challenge—**it is a sin**.

Hebrews 3:12 puts it plainly: *"Take heed, brethren, lest there be in any of you an evil heart of* **unbelief***, in departing from the living God."*

For years, I lived in unbelief without even realizing it. I believed in God, attended services, and prayed, but deep down, I thought I had to *'do'* to get God to *'act.'* Whether it was healing, finances, or relationships, my mindset was one of striving—trying to earn God's blessings by my actions. I did not yet understand the depth of what Jesus meant when He said, *"It is finished."*

This morning, my husband and I were talking about healing, but the conversation expanded into a deeper recognition of how **everything**—our finances, our relationships, and every area of life—was already provided for. It was not just healing that Jesus secured for us; it was total restoration. I had been living as if I needed to persuade God to take care of things for me, rather than resting in the truth that all of this was taken care of at the Cross. I just needed to trust Him, believe Him, and learn to rest in that truth. Once I received this revelation it did not just change how I prayed; it changed how I lived.

Faith and Unbelief: The True Barrier to Breakthrough

Believers desire healing, provision, and restoration. They pray and trust God's power—yet they struggle to see results. Why?

It is not a lack of faith. Every believer already has faith—the same faith that brought them salvation. *Romans 12:3* says, *"God has dealt to each one a measure of faith."* Salvation itself comes by believing in Jesus, not by feeling something first or praying enough times. Healing and every promise of God are received the same way—by faith.

The issue is not needing more faith; it is unbelief blocking the faith you already have. *Matthew 17:20* tells us that even faith as small as a mustard seed can move mountains. Faith holds limitless power, but unbelief weakens its effect. This is the truth Satan desperately wants to keep hidden. The breakthrough is not about striving for more faith—it is about removing what hinders it. **That** is what *transforms your understanding*.

This Kind Goeth Not Out but by Prayer and Fasting – A Deeper Look

The verse *"Howbeit this kind goeth not out but by prayer and fasting."* **Matthew 17:21** is **often** misunderstood. Many assume Jesus was referring to a stronger type of demon, but in context, He was addressing the disciples' unbelief—**not** the power of the demon itself.

Let us break it down clearly:

1. The Story Behind the Statement (Matthew 17:14-21 & Mark 9:14-29)

- A desperate father brings his demon-possessed son to Jesus' disciples for healing. The boy suffers from violent seizures, and the demon repeatedly tries to kill him.

- The disciples try to cast it out, but nothing happens.

- The father then turns to Jesus and says, *"I brought him to Your disciples, but they could not cure him."* (**Matthew 17:16**).

- Jesus immediately rebukes them: *"O faithless and perverse generation, how long shall I be with you?"* (**Matthew 17:17**).

- He then casts out the demon instantly, and the boy is healed.

Afterward, the confused disciples ask, *"Why could we not cast it out?"* (**Matthew 17:19**).

Jesus answers in two key parts:

1. *"Because of your unbelief"* (**Matthew 17:20**). → He makes it clear that their lack of faith was the problem, not the strength of the demon. But notice—He does not say they had *no* faith at all. They had faith, or else they would not have attempted to cast out the demon in the first place. The issue was that unbelief was present *alongside* their faith, weakening its effect. It was not the *size* of their faith that failed them, but the presence of doubt that undermined it.

2. *"This kind does not go out except by prayer and fasting."* (**Matthew 17:21**). → But *what kind* was He talking about?

2. Was Jesus Talking About a Stronger Demon?

Believing *'this kind'* refers to a powerful, stubborn demon **does not** line up with the rest of Scripture.

Here is why: Jesus had already given the disciples power over ALL demons.

*"Behold, I give you authority… over **ALL** the power of the enemy."* (**Luke 10:19**).

They had already cast out demons before (**Luke 10:17**). Why would this one be different? Jesus Himself cast it out without fasting first. If fasting was required for this type of demon, why did Jesus not fast before commanding it to leave? He simply spoke, and it was gone. Nowhere else in Scripture does Jesus say demons require fasting to be removed. If some demons were stronger than others, He would have taught the disciples a different method. Instead, He focused on faith.

3. *'This Kind'* = **A Kind** of Unbelief

Jesus was not referring to a special category of demons—He was talking about a specific kind of unbelief that only leaves through fasting and prayer.

There are three main types of unbelief:

1. Lack of knowledge – Not knowing what God has promised. (**Hosea 4:6** – *"My people are destroyed for lack of knowledge…"*)

Under the New Testament, this verse still applies, but in a different way. Rather than rejecting the Old Covenant law, unbelief now comes from **not knowing what Christ has already provided**. Many believers struggle, not because God is withholding, but because they lack understanding of His finished work. **Romans 10:17** confirms this: *"Faith comes by hearing, and* *hearing by the word of God."* The solution to this kind of unbelief is gaining **revelation knowledge** of God's grace through Jesus Christ.

2. Wrong teaching – Believing something contrary to God's Word. (Like thinking God is trying to teach you something or believing that healing *will happen* instead of **knowing** that it is already done.)

3. Natural unbelief – When what we *see, feel, and experience* contradicts what God says.

The disciples faced natural unbelief in this situation. They saw the violent manifestations of the demon—how it threw the boy into seizures and convulsions—and it shook their faith. They had faith, but their natural senses overpowered it.

That is why Jesus told them fasting and prayer were needed—**because those are the tools that break natural unbelief and sharpen our spiritual perception.**

4. Why Fasting and Prayer?

Fasting does not make God move—**it removes distractions** so that we can **hear Him** more clearly.

• Prayer connects us to God, increasing our sensitivity to His Spirit.

• Fasting disconnects us from the flesh, weakening the influence of doubt and fear.

Together, they sharpen our faith so we can walk in the authority we already have. This is one of the key truths that many overlook, yet it directly impacts healing. When I realized this, I remember saying, "*God, that is it!*"—it was as if a light switched on.

People need to grasp this revelation, because once they do, it changes how they approach healing entirely.

5. How Does This Apply to Us Today?

Many believers struggle to resist the devil, receive healing, or walk in faith—not because they lack authority, but because unbelief blocks it. Have you ever prayed for something and then immediately doubted? That is unbelief at work. The issue is not a lack of power but unbelief undermining the power you already have.

The Solution?

• **Consistent prayer keeps you spiritually aligned** – The more you stay connected to God, the more your faith is strengthened.
• **Fasting weakens the flesh and removes distractions** – It silences the doubts that come from relying on what you see, feel, and experience.
• **Feeding on the Word replaces unbelief with truth** – Faith comes by hearing (**Romans 10:17**). The more you meditate on God's promises, the harder it is for doubt to take root.
• **Acting on faith reinforces what you believe** – Faith is not just knowing the truth; it is stepping out in it. The more you act in faith; the more unbelief loses its grip.

The Power Was Already in Them (And in Us!)

The disciples already had the authority to cast out demons. Their failure was not due to the demon's power—it was due to **their own** wavering faith. They allowed what they saw in the natural world to overshadow what they knew to be true in the Spirit. Fear crept in, blocking their ability to heal. That is why Jesus did not need to fast before casting it out—He had zero unbelief.

The same is true for us. When we face situations where it feels like *nothing is changing*, it is not because the enemy is stronger. It is because doubt and fear are getting in the way. Fasting and prayer do not force God's hand. They remove unbelief so that we can step into the authority we already have.

Fasting Under the New Testament of Grace

Many believers view fasting through an Old Testament lens, focusing on rituals rather than its true purpose. Under grace, fasting is not about earning God's favor but about removing distractions and growing in spiritual awareness.

1. What is Biblical Fasting?

At its core, fasting is the intentional act of denying the flesh to focus on God. Fasting is not about making God move—it moves you into deeper awareness of Him. It is not a tool to prove righteousness, but a way to silence distractions and strengthen faith.

2. Fasting: Old vs. The New

In the Old Testament, fasting was often tied to mourning, repentance, or seeking deliverance (**Nehemiah 1:4, Esther 4:16**). But in the New Testament, everything changed:

- Jesus declared, *"It is finished"* (**John 19:30**).

- We no longer fast to earn God's attention but to grow in awareness of what we already have.

- The early church fasted before making decisions (**Acts 13:2-3**), not to receive blessings but to walk in alignment with God's will.

This is why Jesus said: *"But the days will come when the bridegroom will be taken away from them, and then they will fast."* (**Matthew 9:15**)

He was saying that after His ascension, fasting would still have a place—but not as a religious ritual. Instead, it would be about drawing near to Him in faith, not striving for what He has already freely given.

3. Should We Still Fast Today?

Yes—but not as a religious obligation. Fasting now strengthens faith, removes distractions, and enhances spiritual sensitivity. The early church continued to fast, but notice how different it was:

They fasted before **making decisions**. (**Acts 13:2-3** – *Before sending Paul and Barnabas, they fasted and prayed.*)

They fasted to minister to the Lord, not to get something from Him. (**Acts 14:23**– *Appointing elders through prayer and fasting.*)

What is the difference?
• They were not fasting for deliverance; they had already been delivered in Christ.
• They were not fasting for favor; they already had God's favor.
• They fasted to hear God more clearly, not to convince Him to speak.

4. What About the Daniel Fast and Old Testament Fasts?

The Daniel Fast was not about drawing closer to God but about rejecting defiled food. Old Testament fasting rituals no longer apply under grace. If done today, fasting should be about aligning with Christ, not striving to earn something from God.

5. How Should We Fast Under Grace?

Fasting can take many forms:

1. Food Fast (Traditional) – Abstaining from food for a period (e.g., one meal, a day, multiple days).
2. Social media/Entertainment Fast – Stepping away from distractions that consume time and attention.
3. Selective Fast – Cutting out specific foods or habits to focus more on prayer.
4. Lifestyle Fasting – Consistently choosing to remove distractions that weaken faith.

Anything that competes for your attention over God can be fasted from.

6. What Happens When We Fast?

- Faith is strengthened. (**Romans 10:17**)
- Spiritual sensitivity increases.
- Unbelief is broken.
- Authority in Christ becomes clearer.

Fasting is not about waiting for God to provide what He has already given—it is about removing the obstacles that keep us from walking in it.

The Power Switch

John 14:12 says, *"Verily, verily, I say unto you, He that believeth on me, the works that I do shall he do also; and greater works than these shall he do; because I go unto my Father."*

This verse is one of the most misunderstood today, yet the truth behind it is life changing. Jesus was not making an empty statement—He was giving believers a direct insight into the authority they now have.

When Jesus ascended, He sent the Holy Spirit to empower every believer. Though His earthly ministry lasted just three and a half years, His message has continued for over 2,000 years through Spirit-filled believers. With technology, books, and global ministries, the gospel has reached more people than ever before. This is the *'greater'* impact Jesus spoke of—the expansion of His kingdom through those who carry His Spirit.

Greater works does not mean outdoing Jesus—let us be real: you do not get much **greater** than raising the dead! It is not about surpassing Him in power but about the reach and multiplication of His works through believers across the world.

But here is what gets missed: *Jesus did not say only preachers or teachers would do these works—He said anyone who believes in Him.* This is where so many Christians struggle.

The Power Given to Every Believer

John 14:12 declares: *"He that believeth on me, the works that I do shall he do also."* Jesus was not speaking only to the twelve disciples—He was speaking to every believer who would come after them. This means that anyone who has faith in Him and is filled with the Holy Spirit is now equipped to do the same work He did.

When Jesus walked the earth, He healed the sick, cast out demons, raised the dead, and demonstrated authority over nature itself. He calmed storms, multiplied food, and brought sight to the blind. These were not just acts of power but demonstrations of the *kingdom* of God at work. He was showing us what is possible when a person is fully surrendered to the Spirit of God.

Now, He has given that same power to every believer. The Holy Spirit is not a lesser version of what was in Jesus—it is the same Spirit that raised Him from the dead (**Romans 8:11**). That means every believer has the authority to lay hands on the sick and see them recover (**Mark 16:17-18**), cast out demons, and walk in supernatural provision. We can speak with wisdom beyond our natural understanding, walk in boldness without fear, and live in the full assurance that we are not victims in this world—we are more than conquerors (**Romans 8:37**).

This is where the power exchange happens. The moment you stop seeing yourself as waiting on God to act and start believing that God has already equipped you, everything shifts.

Spirit-Led

A believer's strength comes from one source—the Holy Spirit. Without Him, you are defenseless. Jesus promised us this **gift** in **John 14:16-17**: *"And I will pray the Father, and He shall give you* *another Comforter, that He may abide with you forever; even the Spirit of truth; whom the world cannot receive, because it seeth Him not, neither knoweth Him: but ye know Him; for He dwelleth* **with you**, *and* **shall be in you**.*"*

When Jesus ascended, He did not leave us without help. He sent His Spirit to dwell within us, equipping every believer to continue His work. Through Him, you receive wisdom, boldness, and divine influence to stand firm in what has already been given. Without knowing the One who lives within us, we *struggle* to step into the spiritual dominion that belongs to us.

Knowing the Person of the Holy Spirit

The Holy Spirit is not an abstract force or a distant presence. He is God, living within us. Let that truth settle: *the Almighty Creator of the heavens and earth now resides in every believer.*

For years, when I prayed, I saw Him as distant—high above in the sky, separate from me, someone who might or might not choose to hear my prayers. I could not see Him for who He truly was: a part of me, living and dwelling on the inside. You hear this truth all your life, and you read the Scriptures, but it does not fully sink in until you begin walking in divine authority. Only then does the veil lift, revealing what it truly means to have the Spirit of God within you.

Think about this: the same One who raised Jesus from the dead now resides *within you* (**Romans 8:11**). He is not waiting somewhere to be called down or to fill a certain place. He is present, active, and working within you. **This understanding is life changing.** He is the source of strength, wisdom, and guidance—not a force you strive to reach, but the One leading us from within.

Jesus called Him our Comforter and Helper—the One who strengthens and directs us (**John 14:26**). He is the Spirit of Truth, revealing God's Word and empowering us to live by it (**John 16:13**).

Acts 1:8 declares, *"But ye shall receive power, after that the Holy Ghost is come upon you."* This strength does not originate from us—it comes from His presence within us. And that, too, is a relief—it shifts the weight off what I can or cannot do and places it on the One who can do all things. That is why I no longer question whether someone *will be* healed when I lay hands on them. I lay hands **knowing** they *are* healed.

The enemy works hard to keep believers unaware of their dominion because he knows an awakened Christian is dangerous to his kingdom. The moment you awaken to what has been placed within you, your perspective shifts.

It is all about the authority you carry. But that authority is not just in your actions—it is in your words. That is why what you speak either activates God's truth or it is reinforcing the enemy's lies—whether you realize it or not. The words you say either align you with God's power of gives the enemy a foothold.

The Power of Words

Every word spoken has the potential to either **build up** or **tear down**. So often, people speak out of the emotions they are experiencing in the moment. But as soon as those thoughts turn into words, they release either life or death—over someone else or even over themselves, whether spiritually or physically. That is how powerful words are, yet some move through the day without truly grasping the weight of what they say.

I have watched countless times as people profess one thing, only to turn around and say another that directly contradicts scripture—immediately negating their healing. It is not that you lack *enough* faith; the issue is that you believe the wrong thing.

Your words must align with scripture. Pay attention to what you say—because if it is not in agreement with scripture, it agrees with the enemy.

Do you 'Speak Things into Existence'?

We often hear the phrase *"Speak it into existence,"* but does the Bible teach this? Some cite **Romans 4:17**, which says God *"calleth those things which be not as though they were."* However, this refers to **God's** power, not ours. Only He creates from nothing—we operate in faith based on what He has already provided.

This does not mean our words lack power. **Proverbs 18:21** remind us that our words align with either faith or fear, life, or destruction. That is why we must be careful how we teach faith-filled speech:

- Instead of *"Speak it into existence,"* say *"Speak in agreement with God's Word."*
- Rather than *"I am rich,"* declare *"God is my provider, and He supplies all my needs"* (**Philippians 4:19**).
- Instead of *"I will never be sick,"* stand on **Isaiah 53:5**: *"By His stripes, I have been healed,"* trusting in His timing.

Our words should always reflect what God has spoken—not just our desires apart from His plan.

Breaking the Habit of Speaking Fear

It took me a long time to break free from saying things like: *"I have a cold," "my head hurts,"* or *"I'm in pain."* Years, in fact. Not weeks—years.

People claim it takes just a few weeks to break a habit, but research by Dr. Phillippa Lally at University College London found that, on average, it actually takes at least two months—sometimes much longer—for a new habit to become automatic. That told me something: this was not just a habit; it was a way of life.

Just last night, I felt pressure building in my head. I started sneezing, and immediately, the thought hit me:

"I'm catching that flu that's going around."

But right away, I recognized it as a lie from Satan. It sounds almost too simple, but let me tell you—learning to consistently recognize Satan's attacks took me a long time and that was studying every single day with this mindset:

"I am already healed."

And as I sit here this morning writing, I am symptom-free—no clogged head, no sneezing, nothing. Because I refused to come into agreement with Satan's lies by saying *"I am catching a cold."*

When I was twelve, my friend gave me a pamphlet titled *Hung by the Tongue*. It seemed insignificant at the time, but its simple truths about the power of words stayed with me. Decades later, those lessons profoundly shaped how I view the connection between our speech and our ability in Christ.

My grandmother also taught me the importance of speaking life. One day, as she asked me to do something I quickly replied, *"I can't,"* and she immediately corrected me: **"There is no such thing as 'I can't.'"** She was not just teaching vocabulary; she was teaching me that *our words shape our reality*. When you say you cannot, you close the door to possibilities. But when you speak with confidence, you align yourself with God's truth and open the door to *growth and breakthrough*.

The Truth About Satan's 'Power'

"Be sober, be vigilant; because your adversary the devil walks about like a roaring lion, seeking whom he may devour." (**1 Peter 5:8**)

That should tell you something. Satan may not be a lion, but he sure acts like one, always looking for an opportunity to devour you.

But here is the point: it is all an act.
- He is not powerful.
- He has no real authority or power.
- His only weapon is deception.

And the moment you stop falling for it, he loses every ounce of control. He has no power.

Speaking in Faith, Not Denial

When I say, *"I don't claim sickness,"* I am not claiming that my words alone have the power to prevent sickness. Instead, I am declaring my faith in God's protection and healing.

I refuse to come into agreement with fear or sickness because I know what the Word of God says about my health. This is not about denying reality—it is about choosing to align my words with faith rather than fear.

Understanding this truth does not weaken the power of words—it strengthens it.

Real power does not come from trying to force reality to change with words alone. It comes from speaking in faith and agreement with what God has already promised.

A Personal Testimony

In 2023, my Mama suffered a stroke. My husband and I walked in on her mid-stroke while she was in the hospital, and the shock of that moment left me traumatized for lack of a better word. I called my sister, and she rushed to the hospital, where we found Mama unable to talk, walk, or move anything on her right side. We were devastated. I reached a point where I could hardly function—emotionally.

The time had come to leave the hospital, but we did not want to leave Mama. Every part of me resisted walking away, but I was on the verge of a breakdown, and my husband recognized it. I was traumatized and overwhelmed. No matter how hard I tried, I could not get the image of her having a stroke out of my mind or shaking off the thought that she was dying at that moment. My husband saw what I could not—how much it was breaking me—and insisted on staying with her overnight. I do not even remember exactly what it was he said that finally persuaded me, but I know it had to have been God leading him.

The next morning, he called me with unexpected news: *"Lee, she can say my name."* The doctors had done what they could, but their outlook remained grim. Later that morning, they told us she likely would not make it through the day. My daughter even recorded the conversation, capturing the doctors' consensus that her survival was improbable. They described her as one of the *'worst cases'* they had seen, considering her numerous health complications. After hearing their report, I thanked them politely but firmly, saying, *"Now I need to go talk to God."* I left the ICU and went to the lobby to pray. My heart was heavy as I poured out every fear, doubt, and tear before Him. Before stepping back through those double doors to the ICU, I paused and said, *"God, I've talked to You, but now I need to hear from You."* His response was clear: *"Whose report are you going to believe?"*

The Holy Spirit reminded me of **Isaiah 53:1**: *"Who hath believed our report? And to whom is the arm of the Lord revealed?"* I held on to that truth as I returned to Mama's room whereby this time she was able to utter a few words. When I walked in, her first words were, *"I want coffee."* I smiled and told her, *"Ole girl, if you give God just a little more time, you'll be drinking coffee."* Hours later, the nurse called into the lobby where I sat with my sister, daughter, and niece to share the news—Mama had passed the swallowing test and was drinking coffee.

The following months we faced many highs and many lows. My sister would often remind me of what the Holy Spirit had spoken to me that day in the hospital: *"Whose report are you going to believe."* His Word sustained us. Over the following days and months, she regained her speech, started walking again, and even returned to driving. The Holy Spirit had guided me, strengthened my faith, and reminded me of God's Word. Mama lived another year after that. Though she later went home to the Lord, her recovery was a testimony to the power of the Holy Spirit.

A Flashlight Without Batteries

The enemy does not respond to our human strength or effort. He recognizes only the authority of Christ within us. In the introduction, I mentioned the story in **Acts 19:13-16**, where the seven sons of Sceva tried to cast out a demon without truly knowing Jesus or the Holy Spirit. The demon replied, *"Jesus I know, and Paul I know; but who are you?"* Without the Holy Spirit, they were powerless.

The same is true today. Our authority does not come from our own ability—it comes from knowing the One who lives within us. Walking in that authority requires more than just knowledge; it requires daily fellowship with the Holy Spirit. When you stay connected to Him, you learn to speak in alignment with His truth and step into the dominion Christ has given. **Even the enemy recognizes the difference between a believer who merely knows about Jesus and one who truly walks in His authority**.

Imagine a flashlight without batteries. The power to produce light does not come from the flashlight itself but from the energy inside it. In the same way, you cannot operate in the **fullness** of your authority on our own—it comes from the Holy Spirit within you. When you are filled with His Spirit and speak His truth, the power of Christ shines through you, and the enemy must respond in defeat. Without that power, just like the sons of Sceva, we are defenseless.

Conclusion: The Power Resides Within You

The Holy Spirit is not distant—He lives within you. He is the source of your spiritual authority and the power with which you overcome the enemy. When you know Him, you stop begging God for what He has provided and start walking in boldness, living as the victorious child of God you were created to be.

Every word you speak has the power to build or destroy. When you walk in the Spirit and use your words wisely, you step into the divine power that Jesus has given you.

The question is —do *you know Him*?

When you do, the enemy will no longer ask, *"Who are you?"* Instead, he will flee as in **James 4:7** reminds us—recognizing the authority of Christ within you.

That is authority.

That is power.

That is dominion.

Satan's Tug of War

Pulled by Doubt, Pushed by Pride

The earliest I can remember my desire to learn about healing began in the late 1990's. I have numerous books and notes on scriptures dating back to that time. My studying went on and off over the years, but everything shifted when my husband, Mark, was diagnosed with liver cancer. It was after his surgery that my desire to understand God's promise of restoration really began to grow. One thing about Satan—he always oversteps. If he had left well enough alone, I probably would not have dug as deep as I did. But after his procedure, he got so sick at Duke Hospital that I began to wonder how he would make it through. I will never forget the moment in that hospital room when the thought hit me: *"There has to be more to healing than just praying and hoping."* Mark was so sick, and even though family and friends were praying back home—prayers I knew sustained us—I felt in my heart that there was something more.

My mind kept going back to my childhood when Mama used to take us to revivals in different places—tent revivals, church services, and more. I remember watching healings take place and demonic spirits being cast out. One event that stood out happened at *The Café* or *Corner Grill*. Revival meetings were held there, and one night, they prayed a demon out of a woman. Afterward, the ones praying wrapped something in a tissue and handed it to me and my two cousins.

They told us to flush it down the commode. We could not have been older than 10 or 12, but we witnessed it. I do not recall what was in the napkin or why it was given to us, but we did what we were told.

As time passed, The Café meetings eventually stopped. But as I got older, I noticed a shift in a lot of different churches. During services, children were now being removed whenever a demon was being cast out. The explanation was always, *"It could enter them— they're too young to understand."* When did we stop commanding demons and start fearing them? Jesus never removed people; He commanded demons to leave them. He cast *'them'* out.

How did this shift happen? Over time, that approach and my own lack of understanding led me to develop that fear. I did not realize it at the time, but in those early years, I was beginning to learn about authority. Sadly, that fear created a barrier to understanding it fully.

After Mark's surgery, I began to search the scriptures continually, looking for answers to my question: *"There has to be more to healing than just hoping and praying."* The truth was, most of the time, it felt like begging and praying. That is when I started digging more into teachings on healing and spiritual authority. The teaching that impacted me most was from Curry Blake. At first, it was hard to follow—not because I did not understand it, but because it challenged so many of my traditional beliefs. Yet I kept studying because the evidence was undeniable: lives were being transformed. *"If this were deception, why would it lead to healing?"* I thought.

Then it hit me —I sounded just like the Pharisees in **Matthew 12:24** when they accused Jesus of casting out devils by Beelzebul's power. I did not agree with them, but I realized how much my traditional beliefs had shaped my thinking. **I was struggling to accept what was right in front of me.**

Breaking the Religious Mindset

It is important to recognize the misrepresentation that some TV evangelists receive. How often do you hear people say, *'You better be careful about those preachers—they're just in it for the money'?* While there are, of course, some who misuse their influence, you cannot let that stereotype keep you from receiving truth. If I had let that mindset control me, I would have missed life-changing teachings from men of faith like Lester Sumrall, Smith Wigglesworth, Curry Blake, Andrew Wommack, Creflo Dollar, and Kenneth E. Hagin.

Creflo Dollar made a significant shift in his teachings, publicly stating that he no longer preached tithing as a requirement under the law but instead embraced giving under grace. In a 2022 sermon, he acknowledged that some of his previous teachings on tithing were incorrect, emphasizing that believers should give out of a heart of gratitude rather than obligation.

This marked a broader shift in his ministry toward focusing more on grace rather than Old Testament law-based teachings. However, his transition has been met with mixed reactions—some applauding his change, while others questioning why it took so long. He still teaches prosperity, but with a stronger emphasis on grace rather than legalistic giving.

I remember one evening when my cousin sent me a link to one of his teachings on *Spiritual Authority*. The message was so powerful, revealing the depth of what resides within us, that I ended up listening to it at least three or four more times.

These teachers helped shatter my mindset of falsehood—that we are still bound under the Old Testament law—revealing instead that the Old Testament was a **shadow** of the New. Holding on to my religious traditions instead of biblical truth had kept me in spiritual bondage.

Stepping Into the New Covenant of Grace

I continued to become more and more intrigued by Curry Blake's testimony of seeing God's power firsthand. According to his testimony, his daughter fell from a second-story window onto a concrete patio. When he found her, she had no signs of life—no breath or heartbeat.

He prayed over her for approximately 30 minutes, repeatedly declaring, *"In the name of Jesus, you will live and not die."* After this time, she expelled a strong breath, spewing blood, and regained consciousness. Medical professionals later confirmed she had been clinically dead for at least 30 minutes.

He had witnessed countless, undeniable transformations. At first, I approached his teachings with skepticism, but I could not argue with the results. It was not the message of grace that was difficult to grasp—it was how deeply it challenged my long-held traditions. Yet, something kept drawing me back.

I think the defining moment for me came when I reached a boiling point in suffering. I was sick and tired of being sick and tired, feeling like I could not break free from the rat race of struggles and yet here it was testimony after testimony of breakthrough, showing me that freedom was possible. The more I listened, the more I recognized the truth in what he was teaching. Everything he taught aligned with the New Testament of Grace, yet breaking free from my Old Testament mindset of performance felt like the ultimate battle.

But the more I wrestled with it, the more I realized I had a choice: **cling to tradition or step into truth.** That choice became clear when I finally began to grasp the reality of the New Covenant of Grace. I did not just keep studying—I started applying what I learned. I began praying for people, not pleading for healing, but **declaring** that they were healed—not because of me, but because of Christ within me.

At first, I did not witness any major miracles like raising the dead, but I saw small changes. As my understanding of spiritual dominion grew, so did the manifestations of healing. I laid hands on my children for pain, and it would instantly leave. The same happened with my husband and me as I continued to learn to walk in dominion. By this time when I prayed for others it was with the understanding they were already healed. Some may question why they have not personally witnessed healing or breakthroughs. That is a natural response; it comes from looking through the lens of the **carnal mind**—one that relies on sight rather than truth. But let me be clear—**faith is not based on what you see.** If you rely on sight, you will always ask questions. But when you walk in faith, you align with what God has already done.

Growing in belief is a continuous journey. The goal is not merely to operate in the gifts described in **1 Corinthians**, but to walk in the fullness of the Spirit. It is not about chasing manifestations—it is about knowing Him. And as belief deepens, the manifestations will follow. Jesus believed it, *so I do too.*

Satan's Strategy: Pulling You Back or Pushing You Forward

Here is the thing. This is where Satan tries to trap you.

While you are learning to walk in the dominion Christ has given you, he will try to pull you back with thoughts like:

"You don't see healing."
"People will think you're a fake."
"No one will believe you."

Then, once you start seeing results, he will push you the other way with thoughts of pride:

"Oh, you've got it."
"Others don't understand their authority, but you do."

That is a lie straight from the pit of hell. Paul himself said, *"I claim to know nothing save Jesus Christ."*

And here is the main point: It is not about what you know or what you can do—it is about Christ and the dominion He has given you.

Looking for Proof

Some people hesitate to step into the fullness of grace because they **wait for proof.** They watch others, looking for miracles and manifestations to determine whether grace is real. But here is something to consider:

1. **If you find yourself constantly looking at whether someone else is walking in power, ask yourself—are you?** It is easy to look at others and say, *"Well, I don't see them performing miracles,"* but if that is your standard, then you also must ask yourself—are you seeing them in your own life? If not, then the real question is not whether grace works—it is whether **you** are truly walking in it. Instead of looking outward, start seeking His truth within. When you begin walking in grace, the manifestations follow—not because you are searching for them, but because they flow naturally from a life surrendered to Him.
2. **You may have the same mindset as those in Nazareth—Jesus' own hometown—where He said, "a prophet is without honor."** They could not receive from Him because they refused to believe He was who He said He was, just as many reject grace today. Why? Because of traditional beliefs that make them blind to it. Jesus addressed this mindset when He said,
"You make the Word of God of none effect through your tradition" **(Mark 7:13)**.

Many rejects grace not because it is not true but because it challenges what they have always known.

3. **You might have a Pharisee mindset—one that looks for something to disprove rather than something to believe.** The Pharisees saw miracles firsthand and still did not believe. They clung to their religious framework so tightly that even undeniable proof could not change their minds.
4. **Or perhaps, it is all of the above.**

Here is the truth—we are all growing in grace. **It is not a competition to see who gets there first.** Grace is not measured by outward signs alone, and it is certainly not a race to prove who is more anointed.

Many take the scripture *"You will be known by the fruit you bear,"* to mean visible miracles or manifestations, but **that is not what Jesus was saying**. He was not pointing to outward signs— He was pointing to the fruit of the Spirit.

So, what is the fruit of the Spirit?

It is not about how many people you have healed or whether you have seen a supernatural sign. It is also not about religious performance—how many good works you have done, how often you go to church, or how much Scripture you can quote. There is nothing wrong with quoting Scripture but the **real evidence of grace at work** in a person's life is this:

- **Love** – Do you love like Christ, even when people do not deserve it?
- **Joy** – Do you have joy that is not shaken by circumstances?
- **Peace** – Does your life reflect the peace of God, or is it filled with fear and anxiety?
- **Patience** – Do you trust God's timing, or are you constantly restless and frustrated?

- **Kindness & Goodness** – Do you reflect the goodness of God through your actions?
- **Faithfulness** – Do you stay firm in truth, or do you waver when it is inconvenient?
- **Gentleness** – Do you correct and lead others with grace, or do you condemn them?
- **Self-Control** – Do you walk by the Spirit, or are you easily led by emotions and impulses?

Paul lays it out plainly in **Galatians 5:22-23**, and there is no way around it—**this is the real measure of spiritual maturity.** The Pharisees saw miracles firsthand yet still did not believe. Jesus Himself said, *"Many will say to me on that day, 'Lord, Lord, did we not prophesy in your name, and in your name drive out demons, and in your name perform many miracles?'"* But His response was sobering: *"I never knew you"* (**Matthew 7:22-23**).

Let that sink in.

Yes, miracles happen, but **they are not the proof of maturity. A life that reflects Christ is.** The fruit of the Spirit is not about **performance**—it is about *transformation.*

Satan will either pull you back with doubt or push you forward with pride, but when you stay **rooted in Christ** and renew your mind daily, you will walk boldly in what has been given.

Chapter 6

Behind Enemy Lines

The ability to discern spiritual battles before they manifest in the natural world is a gift—but it is one you must cultivate. God often warns us ahead of time, but if you are not tuned in to His voice, you may not recognize the warning until it is too late.

The War Unseen

Years ago, long before my son Cainan was born, I had a vivid dream that has stayed with me ever since. I was standing in the fellowship hall of our local church, immersed in laughter and conversation. My daughter, Alina, stood in the middle of it all, still on the edge of her teenage years, smiling, soaking it in, surrounded by her friends.

But as I looked around, I noticed something no one else seemed to see—there were beings among them that did not belong.

These beings were demonic in nature. I just kept staring, disturbed by how they moved unnoticed among the youth. No one saw them, and that troubled me because they were everywhere—watching, lurking. To everyone else, they looked like regular people, blending in as if nothing were wrong. But I could see it—the way they glared, claiming ownership as if to say, *"They're mine."*

I woke up, the dream still as vivid as reality. The following week, I stood before the congregation and shared it, warning them about the dangers young people face—dangers they often do not recognize because they lack discernment.

Looking back, I now realize the youth in the dream did not just represent young people—they symbolized those young in Christ—believers still learning how to discern what they are truly up against.

The Snake on the Step: A Real-Life Warning

Not long after that dream, I had a conversation with Alina that brought the reality of spiritual discernment even closer to home.

She was about fourteen at the time, standing outside, begging me to let her go to the football game with her friends. As she pleaded, I could not shake the uneasy feeling inside me. Instead of simply saying no, I explained this way:

"Imagine you are about to step onto the porch, but just before you do, I stop you. You did not see it, but there was a snake coiled on the step, ready to strike. You were too caught up in talking to notice, but I saw it. I stopped you—not to ruin your plans, but to protect you from what you couldn't see."

She looked at me, puzzled, as I continued.

"This is why I'm telling you that you can't go to the football game with just your friends tonight. It is not that I do not trust you—it is that I see dangers you do not. You may not understand now, but I need you to trust me."

That night, two rival gangs showed up at the game. Afterward, a drive-by shooting took place at a gas station where a lot of the students often gathered after football games. When we heard the news later that week, I turned to Alina and reminded her of our talk about the snake on the step.

"You didn't see the danger, but I did. Just like that imaginary snake, the enemy sets traps we do not always notice. That's why God tells us to be vigilant, to put on the full armor of God, because we're not just wrestling with what we can see—we're up against unseen forces."

That night, Alina understood. She saw that my decision was not about control—it was about protection. More importantly, she learned that not every danger announces itself; some happen secretly.

And that is exactly how the enemy operates. His attacks are rarely obvious. He works through deception, distractions, and unseen traps, hoping to catch us unaware.

Fighting Blind or Fighting Right?

Too often, believers sit unaware, wondering why certain people treat them poorly, failing to realize that Satan is the one at work—not the person—though they may be allowing it. They waste time fighting people instead of recognizing the real enemy is unseen.

One day, my son came to me, frustrated with a friend at school. He could not understand why his friend was acting differently, making choices that directly opposed the Word.

I could see the frustration in his eyes—the kind that comes when you do not understand the battle you are actually fighting.

I reminded him, *"Son, this isn't just about your friend's choices. The enemy is always at work, feeding lies and twisting truth. But instead of getting angry, we have to respond with wisdom. Jesus never ignored sin, but He also never let the enemy bait Him into offense. He spoke truth, but He walked in love."*

When people gossip about you, when they shun you, when they slander you—there is a demonic influence at work behind it. Without spiritual maturity through God's Word, people can become instruments of deception—even believers.

This is why discernment is key. If you do not see the real enemy, you will end up fighting the wrong battle.

Preparing for Battle

Recognizing the enemy's tactics is just the first step—but what good is seeing the battle if you are not armed and ready to fight?

This is not a flesh-and-blood war; it is a spiritual war, and the only way to win is to engage with spiritual weapons. Satan does not respond to emotions—he responds to authority. If you are not prepared, the enemy will have you running in circles, fighting distractions instead of dismantling his schemes.

You do not argue with demons—you cast them out, especially from your mind.

The enemy is not interested in reasoning with you, hearing what you think about him, or even the names you call him. And you do not need his permission to take dominion. Jesus never debated demons—He commanded them to go! (**Mark 1:25**). Stop pleading and start declaring the authority Christ has already given you.

You do not fight spiritual battles with emotions—you fight with the Word of God. Satan wants you to react, to be led by feelings instead of truth. But faith is not based on emotions; it is based on what God has spoken. When Jesus was tempted in the wilderness, He did not engage in conversation—He responded with Scripture. (**Matthew 4:4,7,10**). The Word is your weapon—use it!

You do not react in fear—you stand unshaken in faith.

Fear is Satan's favorite tool because it paralyzes believers from taking action. But faith makes you immovable! **Ephesians 6:16** tells us to take up the shield of faith, which quenches every fiery dart of the wicked one.

This is not the time to sit on the sidelines. You were created to walk in dominion, to stand in authority, and to crush the enemy beneath your feet. The only question is—are you prepared?

Final Thoughts - Will You Be Prepared?

When God warns you, you have two choices—you can listen and be prepared, or you can ignore it and walk into danger blind.

You may not always see the enemy, but that does not mean he is not there.

Jesus was not just informing His disciples that they had authority; He was **commanding** them to use it. **Luke 10:19** is not just a promise; it is an expectation. Scripture repeatedly commands every believer to apply His Word. In the Bible, serpents often represent deception (**Genesis 3:1)** and scorpions represent torment (**Revelation 9:3-5**).

When Jesus declared, *"Behold, I give unto you power to tread on serpents and scorpions, and over all the power of the enemy,"* He was saying that every demonic attack—every deception, oppression, and scheme of the enemy—is under our feet. **Through Christ,** you have been given dominion to walk in victory, crushing Satan's influence, not shrinking back in fear. You have been warned. You have been armed. Now, you have a choice to step forward in faith and crush the enemy beneath your feet, never to walk in fear again.

Winning The War: Before It Begins

Reality Check

Scrolling through social media can feel like a battlefield of defeat. Post after post reflects frustration, anger, and hopelessness. Believers unknowingly speak defeat over their lives, saying:
- *"I can't catch a break."*
- *"I'm cutting toxic people off in the New Year."*
- *"Why does this always happen to me?"*
- *"I guess it was just not meant to be."*
- *"I am always struggling, no matter what I do."*
- *"People always take advantage of me."*
- *"I will never get ahead."*
- *"It's just one thing after another."*

Instead of taking ownership of their thoughts and actions, they shift blame, trapped in a cycle that keeps them from stepping into what Christ has already secured for them.

Winning Starts with Your Thoughts

Before triumph can manifest in your life, it must take root in your mind. **Proverbs 23:7** says, *"For as he thinketh in his heart, so is he."* Your thoughts **shape** your reality. If you constantly see yourself as defeated, unworthy, or incapable, you will live out that narrative. But when you align your thoughts with God's Word, you begin to see yourself as He sees you: victorious, loved, and empowered.

For years, I lived in a cycle of striving, always trying to **earn** what God had already given. My thoughts were filled with doubt and frustration, and it was not **until** I renewed my mind daily with His Word, my outlook was transformed. When you understand that victorious living is not something you achieve but something you receive, your mindset shifts.

Replace Lies with Truth

Satan plants lies, *hoping* they take root in your thoughts. He whispers, *"You'll never overcome this"* or *"You're not good enough for God to use."* But every lie must be countered immediately with scripture. When you hear, *"You'll never overcome this,"* respond with **Romans 8:37**: *"Nay, in all these things we are more than conquerors through Him that loved us."*

Take note: Jesus said the Holy Spirit would remind you of His words in **John 14:26**. If you read scripture daily, He is faithful to bring them back to your memory to use as a weapon. But, and I do not ask this lightly, if you have not renewed your mind to it, then how can He bring back what is not there?

The battle for your life is fought and won in your thought life. The enemy knows that **if** he can control your thoughts, he can control your actions. He may not be able to read your mind, but he can surely influence it—planting doubts, feeding lies, and twisting truth to keep you trapped in fear and defeat. But when you replace his lies with God's truth, you dismantle his schemes **before** they take root.

Now, let us take a step back—do you even recognize when it is Satan speaking to you? We covered this in Chapter 1.

Every negative thought whispered in your mind comes straight from the deceiver:
- *You are fat. You are ugly. You are too skinny. You are unattractive.*
- *You are broke. You will not get ahead. Life is not fair.*
- *Look at how you are being treated. They have rejected you. They are talking about you.*

How often do people get distracted by these thoughts—dwelling on them, replaying them—until they dominate the entire day? That is exactly what Satan wants. If he can keep you focused on lies, you will not walk in truth.

And here is the thing—if you do not already know how to walk in the authority residing in you before the attack comes, simply grabbing a Bible in the moment will not be enough. Satan knows that. The question is, **do you?**

There is no difference between the demon that attacks your mind and the ones being cast out of people. The same authority that drove them out in Scripture is the same authority that silences their whispers in your thoughts. They **all** tremble at the name of Jesus (**James 2:19**). They have no real power—only the illusion of it. The only way they gain ground is when you allow fear to make them seem bigger than they are. But the moment you stand firm in the power of God's Word, they are exposed as weak, defeated, and powerless against you.

We went into depth about the powerlessness of demons and casting them out in Chapter 3, so just to reemphasize: the only power demons have is what people allow them to have. The same Jesus who cast them out of people is the same Jesus inside of you now (**Colossians 1:27**).

- Demons do not get to decide whether they leave—you do.

- Fear is their only weapon, but it only works if you believe their lies.
- When you recognize their tactics and take authority, they have no choice but to flee!

If you would not allow a demon to take over your home, why let it take over your thoughts? The power is already in you—not in the Bible you grab in a panic, but in the living Word inside your Spirit!

Some assume that reading the Bible alone is enough, but Satan knows scripture too—he has had over 2,000 years to learn it word for word. He does not care how much you read—it is how much you **discern** that threatens him.

And that is exactly why works can't sustain you. If human effort alone could give victory, most believers would not struggle—because many have a heart to do what is right.

But effort without faith still leads to frustration. It is not about striving—it is about abiding.

It is not about how much you do—it is about how much you **believe** He is working through you.

Discernment comes from abiding. Strength comes from knowing—not just reading. Victory comes from **believing**—not just trying.

And Satan fears that more than anything.

The Armor of God

A Call to Walk in Authority

Spiritual battles are won **before** they ever manifest in the natural. That is why God gave us armor—not for decoration, but for action in **Ephesians 6**.

1. **The Belt of Truth** – Truth holds everything together. Be willing to unlearn traditions that do not align with God's Word and replace them with His unchanging truth.
2. **The Breastplate of Righteousness** – Righteousness is not something you earn—it is something you receive (**2 Corinthians 5:21**). Instead of striving to earn it, simply receive it and walk in the confidence of who you are in Christ.
3. **The Shoes of Peace** – You cannot stand firm in battle if you do not know what belongs to you. *It is grace that frees and empowers you to fulfill the law, not the burden of striving to meet it.* Living under the law will always leave you falling short, but living in grace will **cause** you to walk in victory—*peace that surpasses all understanding.*
4. **The Shield of Faith** – Faith grows based on what you feed it. If you barely pray or study, your faith will be weak but as you feed on God's Word daily, your faith will rise in strength. *That is life!*
5. **The Helmet of Salvation** – The mind is the first place the enemy attacks. This is why we renew it daily (**Romans 12:2**). Guard your thoughts because they shape your reality.
6. **The Sword of the Spirit** – The Word is not just for reading—it is for declaring. Jesus did not think about scripture when tempted—He spoke it. What a powerful weapon!

Living in Triumph, Not Just Moments of Breakthrough

Overcoming is not about waiting for one moment of deliverance or getting past one struggle, one setback, or one disappointment after another—it is about living in *sustained* triumph. You gain:

• Freedom from Sin – **Romans 6:14**: *"For sin shall not have dominion over you."* Grace does not excuse sin—it empowers you to walk above it. You do not have to wait for a miracle to overcome sin; God's grace gives you the strength to rise above it every day.

- Strength in Challenges – **Philippians 4:13**: *"I can do all things through Christ which strengtheneth me."* Your strength is not based on your own ability but on the unshakable power of Christ in you. When challenges arise, your focus on Him will carry you through.
- Success in Relationships – **Colossians 3:13**: *"Forbearing one another, and forgiving one another…"* Walking in dominion means **refusing** to let bitterness take root. Relationships are strengthened when you refuse to hold onto grudges. Grace in your heart creates peace in your relationships, not because you *'should'* forgive, but because something in you shifts. You will find that letting go of hurt is not about forgetting—it is about releasing what no longer has the power to control you. When you experience grace, it becomes easier to extend it to others, even in your most painful relationships.

Living in **sustained** triumph means you no longer live in the momentary victory of overcoming struggles, but in the continuous power of grace, strength, and peace that Christ gives. This is not just about feeling better for a moment—it is about a lasting transformation that changes you from the inside out. This is your new way of life—a life of perpetual victory, not just occasional breakthroughs.

Dominion: Your Birthright

Living in triumph is your birthright as a child of God. *This is your new normal.* You are no longer bound by circumstances. *The moment you begin to receive the truth of God's Word, you activate a new reality, and your life has no choice but to align with that truth.* It is not just about knowing these truths—it is about them becoming real to you, sinking deep into your heart.

Through Christ, you already have everything you need to walk in strength:

- The dominion of His name.

- The promises of His Word.
- The power of the Holy Spirit within you.

The enemy will do everything in he can to make you feel defeated. But the truth remains—he has already lost.

You were not created to live in cycles of struggle, barely scraping by, waiting for breakthrough after breakthrough. You were created to reign. To walk in dominion. To live in sustained victory, not occasional triumph.

This is not just a hope for the future—it is your reality *now*.

Every battle you face has already been won in Christ. Every stronghold crumbles in the presence of His Word. Every lie the enemy has whispered is silenced when you stand in the authority of who you are.

You are not waiting for freedom—you *have* it. You are not hoping for victory—you *own* it.

'1' Planted

Taking Responsibility

Paul did not say, *"We planted."* He said, *"I planted."* Paul knew that planting seeds was his calling, but he also trusted God for the increase.

1 Corinthians 3:6 *"I have planted, Apollos watered; but God gave the increase."*

Have you ever wondered why people often say, *"We need to be doing this,"* or *"We need to be doing that"* as though making such declarations gives their statements more weight? Paul did not generalize or shift responsibility onto others. He simply acknowledged his role: *I planted.* He understood his calling and acted on it, trusting that an Apollos would come along to water it and God would bring the increase.

Too often, well-meaning believers adopt an Old Testament, performance-based mindset, saying things like, *"God helps those who help themselves."* It is a popular saying, but it is not actually found in Scripture. Statements like this are intended for good, no doubt, meant to encourage devotion and commitment to God. However, the focus remains on what <u>you</u> do rather than what <u>Christ</u> <u>has</u> <u>done</u>. This mindset often leads people to feel guilty for their shortcomings, as if *their failures* are the reason they are not experiencing God's blessings. But it does not negate the fact that the one saying it struggles just as much to keep the law. These words, rather than bringing freedom, only place a burden on others—a burden Christ already carried to the cross. I was one of the loudest voices, standing up and proclaiming, *"We need to be doing this or that,"* believing I was encouraging others. But over time, I realized that mindset came from a place of performance—trying to fulfill expectations or force results. Reaching the point of simply planting, instead of focusing on what others were doing—or not doing—was pivotal.

My husband once asked me about people who say they hear from God and then give others direction based on it. He had noticed how often this happened and wondered where the line was between godly guidance and personal influence. I responded, *"Yes, I believe God reveals things to us according to Scripture, but there's a fine line in how we present it to others."* If our words are focused on what *we* need to be doing, that is a clear sign that *we* are not doing it ourselves. It is like someone trying to sell you a business idea but constantly saying, *'We need to be doing this.'* That tells me you are not doing what you are asking others to do, so why should I listen to the rest of your pitch? Instead, show me how you have overcome, how you have found success, and how I can be empowered to do the same. The moment you point out that I am falling short in every area, and you are too, you have lost me. I need to hear about victory, not just defeat.

God's way is clear: true worship is done in <u>spirit</u> and <u>truth</u>, not in striving or pin pointing failure. When I said things like, *"We need to do better,"* what I was really saying was, *"I'm falling short, and I see that you are too."* Somehow, if I lumped my failures with everyone else's, it felt less like judgment—but it was judgment all the same. Instead of focusing on God's work in my life, I was worried about others *'doing their part,'* as though their perceived shortcomings could somehow derail everything and lead us all astray.

Shifting from Influence to Control

Taking responsibility for what God has called you to do is freeing. But sometimes, without realizing it, people attempt to influence situations in ways that cross the line from encouragement into control. That is where manipulation creeps in—sometimes so subtly that we do not even recognize it. I had a dream that made this reality hit me in a way I had never considered before —showing just how subtle manipulation can be and how easily we can fall into it without realizing.

Witchcraft and Manipulation

Over the years, my dreams have become much more vivid, and their interpretation has grown clearer. This morning, as I woke up, I asked God what my latest dream was about.

In the dream, I was in a group setting where we were all performing small tasks. As a mentor to young women around the age of my daughter, who is now in her late twenties, I moved from one person to another, working alongside them. At one point, I made a simple comment about how much I missed *Jean*, the young woman I had been working with earlier. But it was not just a passing remark—I deliberately said it in a way that gave the impression I preferred Jean over Jill.

The moment I said it, I noticed a shift in the expression of *Jill*, the one I was currently working with. A little later, the instructor asked Jill a question about Jean, and without hesitation, she snapped back in a negative tone. In that moment, I realized what had happened—I had influenced the situation, and it had stirred up envy between them.

When I woke up, I wondered why I would have such a dream. As I asked the Holy Spirit for understanding, He spoke clearly: *Words are not always spoken in a hurtful manner. Sometimes, they are spoken as a way to control the actions of others. That is manipulation. And manipulation is a form of witchcraft.*

This struck me deeply. Anytime a person says or does something in an attempt to control the outcome of a situation, it is manipulation. And manipulation, in and of itself, is a form of witchcraft. It is subtle, often disguised as concern, persuasion, or even love, but at its core, it is about exerting control over others rather than trusting God.

The Bible warns against manipulation, equating it with rebellion and divination. **1 Samuel 15:23** makes this clear: *For rebellion is as the sin of witchcraft, and stubbornness is as iniquity and idolatry. Because you have rejected the word of the Lord, He also has rejected you from being king.* Rebellion—choosing one's own way over God's—is likened to witchcraft because both involve rejecting divine authority in favor of personal control.

Galatians 5:19-21 lists the works of the flesh, including *sorcery* (translated from the Greek *pharmakeia*, which includes witchcraft and manipulation): *Now the works of the flesh are evident, which are: adultery, fornication, uncleanness, lewdness, idolatry, sorcery, hatred, contentions, jealousies, outbursts of wrath, selfish ambitions, dissensions, heresies, envy, murders, drunkenness, revelries, and the like; of which I tell you beforehand, just as I also told you in time past, that those who practice such things will not inherit the kingdom of God.*

Manipulation is a hidden sin that people often justify, but **2 Corinthians 4:2** warns against such deceit: *But we have renounced the hidden things of shame, not walking in craftiness nor handling the word of God deceitfully, but by manifestation of the truth commending ourselves to every man's conscience in the sight of God.* Craftiness, deceit, and twisting words to influence others are all forms of manipulation and should be renounced.

Proverbs 6:16-19 lists behaviors that God hates, many of which are tied to manipulation: *These six things the Lord hates, yes, seven are an abomination to Him: A proud look, a lying tongue, hands that shed innocent blood, a heart that devises wicked plans, feet that are swift in running to evil, a false witness who speaks lies, and one who sows discord among brethren.* Many who manipulate others use lies, deceit, and discord to achieve their desired outcome.

Micah 2:1 also speaks to this: *Woe to those who devise iniquity, and work out evil on their beds! At morning light, they practice it because it is in the power of their hand.* Those who seek control often scheme and plan ways to ensure situations unfold in their favor.

Even jealousy and self-seeking, which often fuel manipulation, are linked to demonic influence. **James 3:14-16** warns: *But if you have bitter envy and self-seeking in your hearts, do not boast and lie against the truth. This wisdom does not descend from above, but is earthly, sensual, demonic. For where envy and self-seeking exist, confusion and every evil thing are there.* When someone uses words or actions to steer people toward a certain response, they are engaging in a form of control that does not come from God.

What the Holy Spirit revealed to me in my dream was a truth many overlooks. Manipulation does not always appear aggressive or forceful. Sometimes, it is as subtle as a carefully placed comment, a strategic silence, or an emotional appeal designed to shift someone's response. Words do not have to be overtly cruel to be manipulative. They can shape actions and emotions in ways that bind people rather than set them free.

Manipulation leaves others feeling uneasy, uncertain, and sometimes even guilty without knowing why. It creates an invisible tension that lingers in the atmosphere, subtly influencing emotions and decisions. Although many may not fully understand they are being manipulated, they can sense when something is off. There is an unspoken awareness that something is not quite right with the person manipulating them. People tend to recognize it deep down, even if they never say anything.

It is these subtle little deceptions from Satan that people yield to, which continuously cause strife, division, and turmoil. Many do not see it in themselves, feeling justified because they believe they are doing it for the betterment of others or even for a church body. But manipulation is never for the greater good—it is about control.

Instead of looking at others and saying, *well, that is so and so who does that,* take a moment to reflect. Have you ever considered whether any of this is present in your own life?

At its core, witchcraft is not just spells and rituals—it is any attempt to control others rather than trust God. It is important to recognize manipulation for what it is and reject it, choosing instead to walk in truth, freedom, and faith in God's sovereignty.

Paul's message is clear: Plant your seeds—not what others expect of you, but what God is teaching you through His Word. **Conviction is powerful because it shines a light on what you are doing, not on what others are doing.** That is the difference between conviction and condemnation. Conviction aligns you with God's Word, revealing your heart so you can walk in freedom. Condemnation, on the other hand, shifts the focus to others' perceived failures, making you a judge when Christ came not to condemn but to save.

"I came not to condemn the world, but that the world through Me might be saved" (**John 3:17**).

His Word convicts so you can grow, but condemnation leads to a cycle of guilt, judgment, and separation. The moment I realized the difference; my heart began to change.

I did not recognize it at the time, but that's exactly how Mama lived out her faith. I am not sure exactly when she stepped into this level of maturity. If you knew her, you would know—'*she was Mama.*' She had her way of telling us what to do, and that was that. But when it came to this Christian Walk, she never told my sister and me what we needed to be doing. Instead, she would come home full of excitement about what she had experienced, and that excitement sparked a thirst for us to know more.

Mama simply spread the good news—planting seeds. And it was not long before someone else came along to water them, shaping us into who *God* was calling us to be. I have lived to reap the increase from those seeds she planted.

Some might say, *"Well, Lee, you were a bit rebellious, and she had to approach you differently."* Looking back, that may be true. But I also believe it had more to do with Mama's understanding of the Word—when He said to preach *Thy Kingdom come* and spread the good news. And because of that, I can now thank God that I was a bit rebellious. Not because I got into trouble and faced consequences—I did—but because, through it all, God still taught me grace, despite who I was.

To be clear, I am not saying rebellion is a good thing. But I am saying this—God can use anything. As I reflected on my own need to grow spiritually and move beyond the mindset of performance, I was about to face a test that would require me to truly live out these lessons.

Recognizing manipulation for what it is allows us to let go of the need to control outcomes and trust God instead. And that brings us back to Paul's example—he planted, and he trusted that Apollos would come to water while God would bring the increase.

The Harvest Will Come

And this is where the power of planting seeds and trusting God's timing really took root in my life. *The harvest* is guaranteed, but it comes in God's perfect timing—sometimes, when you least expect it. My journey of learning to plant, water, and trust Him more deeply was about to be tested in ways I never could have imagined.

This lesson would be put to the ultimate test with my son when he was around 12 years old. Cainan had always been in the top percentage of his class...until now. Getting him through the sixth grade felt like an unbearable weight, crushing me more with each passing day. It got to a point where instead of trying to micromanage or *fix* him or our situation, I had to learn to lean into believing in God's plan and timing.

Here we were midway through the semester, and he was in a struggle, so much that one evening, he sat on my bed, tears streaming down his face, and said words that shattered me:

"Mama, they hate me," he sobbed, referring to his teachers. *"And I hate school."*

In that moment, something inside me broke. I dropped to my knees beside him, sobbing just as hard, unable to find a single word of comfort. I wrapped my arms around him, but I had nothing to offer—no solutions, no reassurance, no hope. Just despair for I too was in a place I could not seem to break free from.

This had been our reality for months. It felt like every effort I made was only adding weight to the burden. I tried everything—meetings, tutoring, endless nights of helping with homework—but nothing seemed to make a difference. I was drowning in frustration, feeling isolated and hopeless. The teachers were doing what they thought was best, but their approach lacked understanding and compassion for the real struggles we were facing. It became clear that they were not fully invested in finding a solution. Then, around Christmas break, I hit a wall. I gave up.

My husband was working out of town. My mama could not help. My daughter—still so young—became my sounding board, forced to carry burdens she should not have had to bear. And me? I felt like I was drowning in helplessness, isolation, and desperation.

I had never felt so alone. And worse, I had never felt so powerless.

One day, I walked over to my sister's house, and she asked, *"how is buddy doing."* I replied, *"I don't care if he quits."* She said, *"What?"* I repeated, *"What part of 'I do not care if he quits' do you not understand?"* She had no idea the depth of what we were up against. She started stepping in to try to help, and within two weeks, she stood on my doorstep crying. *"Lee, I am so sorry. I did not know it was this bad and I don't know how you have done it."* I looked at her with utter gloom on my face and said, *"Na, if you crumble, then what else do I have?"* It was a crushing experience for us all. It was not long after that she called my husband and said, *"Mark, you're going to have to come home, we're losing Lee."*

Cainan had been diagnosed with ADHD, and the only solution the school seemed to offer was medication. The medication left him depressed and slowed his cognitive skills to the point of almost non-functioning. To say I felt defeated was a complete understatement. The teachers still showed little concern beyond complaints that he was disrupting their class or not doing his work. One day, I walked out of their room and said, *"My boy may not excel in your class, but he has something great on the inside of him, although you may not see it yet."*

I began to feel hatred growing in my heart. I had just enough knowledge of the Word to know I could not live my life like that although there were parts of me that felt like I did not care. I repented but the despair I felt remained unchanged. During that time, my mama came to me and said, *"Lee, I do not see him like this. Baby, start speaking over Cainan in how God sees him."* I took her advice and began speaking God's truth over my son. By God's grace, we made it through that year.

The following year, he got a teacher who took the time to build a rapport with him. During a parent-teacher conference, he told me, *"If you'll just let me work with Cainan in my way and work with him accordingly, you'll see a change."* I agreed, and sure enough, he kept his word.

I had been taught the Word from an early age, and now, I had to step out in faith. The seeds my husband and I had planted in Cainan over the years needed to be released. It was time for me to let go and trust that others would come to water them, while God would bring the increase. At that moment, I realized I could not fix his situation or change the teachers. What I didn't understand then was that neither the teachers nor my son's situation were the problem—it was my lack of understanding.

One of our local pastors began working with him at his shop, and one evening, Cainan came home with an unusual look in his eyes. There was a shift—something had changed.

"Mama, he told me"—referring to the pastor—*"'Boy, there is not anything wrong with you, and I know how to work with that,'"* he said, referring to the diagnosis he had been given.

That moment did not just give me hope—it gave Cainan undeniable encouragement. Someone exercising their authority had declared over and to him that he was *okay*—that what the world had labeled as a problem was not a limitation at all.

Looking back, I see now that I had to release the seeds my husband and I had planted in our son's life. What might have seemed like a simple statement to others was life-altering for us. The pastor's words were a reminder that God was already at work, even when I could not see it. That moment deepened my understanding of what it means to plant in faith and trust God for the increase.

The battle often starts in the mind. **2 Corinthians 10:5** urges us to *"take every thought captive to Christ."* During Cainan's challenges, I wrestled with doubt, frustration, and feelings of helplessness. The enemy whispered lies like, *"This will never change,"* or *"You're failing as a parent."* But my mother's advice to speak life over him shifted my focus. Instead of echoing the negative reports, I began declaring God's promises: *"Cainan has the mind of Christ. He is strong, capable, and filled with purpose."*

The transformation was not instant, but it was undeniable. As I spoke life over him, my own thoughts aligned with God's truth, strengthening me to walk this journey with faith. And in time, not only did he graduate, but he also went on to college.

Trusting God to Bring the Increase

Paul did not stress over who would water—he simply planted. And in the same way, I am learning to do the same. Instead of worrying about who is doing what, I am called to plant the seeds God has given me, release them, and trust that in His perfect timing, the increase will come.

My journey with Cainan taught me this truth firsthand—planting requires faith, patience, and the humility to step back. When I finally released my grip and trusted God's timing, the right people came along to water what had already been sown. The increase was never in my hands to begin with.

This shift—from condemnation to conviction—brought me into a deeper understanding of grace. It is not about holding others to a standard we create, but about living in obedience to God's call and allowing Him to work. Instead of saying, *"We need to be doing this"* or *"We should be doing that,"* the better question is, *"Lord, what do You want me to do?"*

Paul did not say, *"We planted."* He said, *"I planted."* He trusted that Apollos would water, and that God would bring the increase. So, must *"we?"*

Taking Charge

As we have learned, planting seeds, and having faith in God to bring the increase requires patience and letting go of control. You learn to stop having faith in your faith and have faith in Jesus' faith. Now, let us explore how healing, like everything else God promises, is part of the abundant life you are called to walk in.

Sickness Is Not Part of God's Plan

Scripture makes it clear—Jesus never made healing optional—He commanded it. His will has not changed.

It is no wonder though, some believers have come to mistakenly think sickness is a tool God uses to teach lessons or punish. This belief contradicts the finished work of the cross.

Isaiah 53:5 declares:

"But he was wounded for our transgressions, he was bruised for our iniquities: the chastisement of our peace was upon him; and with his stripes <u>we are healed</u>."

This scripture addresses *sin* as the subject. Jesus' sacrifice on the cross was not only to secure healing for our bodies but also to heal the brokenness caused by sin. The healing referenced here is rooted in the redemption from sin's consequences. We will explore more about healing from sin in Chapter 10, but for now, it is crucial to understand that healing is a comprehensive provision, addressing both our physical and spiritual restoration.

Why the Shift?

Isaiah foretells the coming Messiah, pointing directly to the place where Jesus bore our sicknesses and pains, both physical and spiritual. So why did the verbiage change from *are healed* in **Isaiah 53** to *were healed* in **1 Peter**? The answer lies in a moment that some overlook—the whipping post.

I remember the first time I truly grasped the significance of the whipping post—it was under one of the teachings of Curry Blake. He emphasized that this was not just a moment of suffering—it was the very place where healing was secured. That understanding stayed with me, and as I studied the Word for myself, I realized how central this moment was to our redemption.

Isaiah 53:5 speaks in the present tense: *"we are healed."* This signifies that when this moment occurs, healing becomes a reality, requiring only belief to activate it.

Matthew 8:17 references the whipping post while Jesus was still ministering on earth, reinforcing that healing was being demonstrated before the cross:
"He himself took our infirmities, and bore our sicknesses." (**Matthew 8:17**, YLT)

But in **1 Peter 2:24**, the language shifts—the whipping had taken place, and healing had been secured. You are not waiting to be healed; you have been healed in the name of Jesus! This healing was not merely declared; it was purchased through His suffering.

The Brutality of Jesus' Beating

The suffering Jesus endured was beyond imagination. His body was not just bruised—it was torn apart. The Roman whip, embedded with shards of bone and metal, did not just leave marks; it lacerated His flesh, stripping muscle from bone. With every strike, His body weakened, His blood poured out, and His pain intensified—but He endured every blow with purpose.

Isaiah 52:14 prophesied the horrifying extent of His suffering:
"As astonished at Thee have been many, (So marred by man His appearance, And His form by sons of men)." (YLT)

His face was unrecognizable. His back was left like a plowed field—**Psalm 129:3** foreshadowed:
"Over my back have ploughers ploughed, they have made long their furrows."

The chastisement of our peace was upon Him, and as blood drenched the ground beneath Him, He pressed forward. Why? Because He saw you. And He saw me. Understand that because of sin, humanity was separated from God—there was no peace between us and Him. To restore that relationship, a price had to be paid. Jesus took our punishment so that you could have shalom—full reconciliation, healing, and rest in God's presence.

- **Romans 5:1** confirms this: *"Therefore, having been justified by faith, we have peace with God through our Lord Jesus Christ."*
- **Colossians 1:20** says Jesus *"made peace through the blood of His cross."*

So, the chastisement for our peace means Jesus endured the suffering that was meant for us.

Knowing the price, He did not turn away—He paid it in full.

Why Rebuild What Jesus Tore Down?

Jesus endured unimaginable suffering for our complete restoration—body, mind, and spirit. But many still live beneath what He provided.

Here is where a believer does His sacrifice an injustice—when they continue to live under the law of performance, as if Jesus did not already declare it insufficient. That was the very reason we were given the New Covenant—to break free from that mindset.

But history shows us that even those who walked with Jesus struggled to let go of the old ways.

Even Peter—who walked with Jesus and saw miracles firsthand—struggled to fully walk in the freedom Christ had given. Paul had to rebuke him in **Galatians 2:11-14** for slipping back into the old law, acting as if it still had authority over them.

That same mistake happens today. Many believers say they trust in Jesus, yet when sickness attacks, they slip into an old mindset—thinking they must earn healing or qualify for it. They mix the old system with the new, treating healing like a reward instead of a finished work.

That is no different than Peter—returning to old ways out of habit, fear, or tradition.

But Galatians makes it clear:
Jesus did not endure the whipping post, the cross, and the weight of all sin just to leave us in bondage to religious duty.

His sacrifice was not just to cover sin—it was to remove the barrier between us and God for the last time.

Moreover, why do some still live like that barrier exist?

When a person clings to old mindsets, thinking they must *'earn'* healing or *'deserve'* breakthrough, they miss the entire point of grace.

His sacrifice wasn't about making us work harder—it was about setting us free.

So let me ask you:

Paul rebuked Peter—Would he rebuke you too?

It is time to stop living as if Jesus partially paid for our freedom.

He finished the work.

It is done.

Now, it is up to us to walk in it.

The Role of Faith in Healing

Healing does not come by hoping or wishing—it comes by faith. **Hebrews 11:1** defines faith as:
"Now faith is the substance of things hoped for, the evidence of things not seen."

It does not say things not *yet* seen. It is *not seen*.

These words are more than just a statement—they are a revelation of true faith. Faith is not about seeing, feeling, or holding onto something physically.

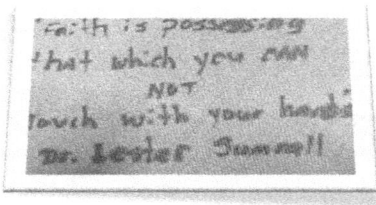

("Faith is possessing that which you cannot touch with your hand." – Dr. Lester Sumrall)

This prayer cloth was not just something I wrote Dr. Sumrall's quote on in 2021. It was a declaration. A constant reminder of faith in action. True faith is not waiting to see the evidence—it is <u>possessing the promise **before** it manifests</u>. That is what this statement means to me, and it is a truth that has shaped my walk with God. It is not passive; it is an unshakable confidence that what God has spoken is more real than what you feel, hear, or experience in the natural.

Look at the centurion in **Matthew 8:5-13**. His servant was still lying in bed, paralyzed and suffering, but he told Jesus, *"Speak the word only, and my servant shall be healed."* The centurion understood that faith does not wait for physical proof—faith sees the promise as reality before it ever manifests.

Or consider the paralytic in **Mark 2:1-12**. His friends tore the roof off a house to lower him to Jesus, and what did Jesus say? *"When he saw their faith..."* Faith was visible. Not because they saw healing happen first, but because they acted, fully convinced that healing would come.

Think about that. **They TORE THE ROOF OFF!**

Make no mistake—when someone goes to another person's house and tears the roof off, they are not hoping to find something inside. They already KNOW it is there.

They were not guessing. They were not wishing. They had faith that Jesus had what they needed, and nothing was going to stop them from getting it.

That is the kind of mindset to have the next time Satan tries to slap you with a lie. Do not hesitate and do not back down. If he tries to tell you are not healed, not forgiven, not free—you come back ready to rip the roof off with the truth of God's Word.

The cross settled it. The very next time, you as a believer, lay hands on someone, know, they are healed. If Satan tries to attack you with thoughts of what if it does not manifest, then just laugh in his face knowing you are no longer carnally minded. You do not *'look'* for manifestation; you believe and walk in it because faith does not wait for proof—it acts on truth.

Think of a landlord who owns a house. If an unauthorized occupant moves in without permission, does the landlord beg them to leave? No! He has the legal right to remove them. He presents the proper documentation, stands on his authority, and the intruder has no choice but to go.

Romans 8:11 declares:

"The same Spirit that raised Jesus from the dead dwells in you."

Healing is not a distant promise—it is your present inheritance. Declare it. Believe it. Possess it.

"I am healed. It is finished."

Sin, Sickness, and The Cross

We have seen that **Isaiah 53** is one of the most powerful chapters in the Bible. It gives us a picture of what Jesus would accomplish through His life, death, and resurrection. This chapter is about living in the fullness of what Jesus has done for us.

The Connection Between Sin and Sickness

This same connection between healing and salvation is seen in **Matthew 9:6**, when Jesus forgave the sins of a paralyzed man before healing him. The religious leaders were outraged, but Jesus was making something clear—if He had the power to forgive sin, then He also had the power to heal sickness.

Healing and forgiveness go hand in hand because **both** were purchased at the cross. Salvation is not just about getting to heaven—it is about complete restoration, body, and soul.

This powerful truth is explored in much more detail in Chapter 17, where we break down why sin no longer condemns us and how grace secures both healing and salvation as part of the same finished work.

The Struggle to Receive Healing

Jesus did not just talk about the Kingdom of God; He demonstrated it. **Luke 10:9** records Him telling His disciples, *"Heal the sick and say, 'The Kingdom of God has come near to you.'"* Healing was a sign that God's rule was breaking into the world, bringing freedom and wholeness. Sickness does not belong in God's

Kingdom. If Jesus told His disciples to announce the Kingdom with power—by healing the sick—then that same commission applies to me.

I began to wrestle with this reality. If the Kingdom of God has come near, why did I continue to live as if it had not? If Jesus demonstrated what it looked like to live under God's rule, then do I continue to accept sickness, fear, and defeat as if they have authority over me? No. The more I thought about it, the more I realized that *the Kingdom of God is not a future event—it is a present reality.* Jesus expected His followers to walk in that same Kingdom power. That means healing is not just something you hope for—it is something you enforce. The question is, do you really believe it? And if you do, what is stopping you from stepping into it?

Some Christians struggle with this because many have been taught that sickness is just a part of life, or worse—that it is something God *allows* to teach a lesson. But that is not what Jesus showed us. When He walked the earth, He healed *everyone* who came to Him in faith. He never once told someone their sickness was *'for a greater purpose."* He never left people in their affliction to *'learn something.'* Every time someone reached for healing, He responded. Why? Because healing is part of redemption. It is God's way of restoring what sin broke.

I remember a time when I was praying for someone who was battling sickness, and deep down, I struggled to believe it would change. I knew what the Bible said, but doubt crept in—what if healing does not come? But that is the mindset of law, not grace. Under the law, we *hope* for healing. Under grace, you *receive* healing. It is not about begging God to move—it is about standing in what Jesus has *already* done.

Healing is not just about physical sickness. People are walking around whole on the outside but broken on the inside. Anxiety, depression, fear, and addiction. These things are just as much a result of sin's curse as sickness in the body. But the cross took care of it *all*. Jesus did not just bear our sins—He bore our pain. **Isaiah 53:6** says, *"The Lord laid on Him the sin of us all."* That means no matter what has tried to **attach** itself to you—whether physical illness, mental torment, or emotional wounds—Jesus already carried it, so you do not have to.

As I neared the publication of this book, my husband came to me with tears in his eyes and said, *"Lee, you have to hear this."* He had just heard a testimony that shook him, and as he began describing it, I could tell it was something powerful. I said, *"Well, put it on now."*

What we watched was a testimony from Andrew Wommack's *Healing is Here* (August 12, 2022, Sessions 14, 15, and 16). If you can, take the time to look it up on YouTube—it is **profound** in explaining how Cindy Mezas overcame cancer simply by speaking and proclaiming God's Word. The testimony starts around the 1:46:00 mark.

(This applies to every struggle we face in life.) This woman took authority and sent Satan's lies straight back to hell—her sickness had no choice but to leave. That is dominion in action.

As we sat watching, I turned to my husband and said, *"I have come to understand that many doctor's reports align with Satan's lies."* And here is the thing—if a person can just stop right there and say, *"No, I do not accept this report because it does NOT align with God's report,"* there would be breakthrough the world could not explain.

It is not that doctors are bad—by no means. But as a believer, you have a choice.

Understanding Sickness as a Spiritual Battle

Whether it is sickness in the body or torment in the mind, it all comes from the same source—the enemy. And just like we do not tolerate sin, you do not have to tolerate sickness either. That is why it is critical to understand healing for what it truly is: a spiritual battle. Think of sickness like a thief in the night—you may not see him enter, but you notice what has been stolen.

1. It is a spiritual attack. Since sickness originates in the spirit realm, you cannot see the attacker with your physical eyes—but that does not make it any less real.

2. It attaches itself to your body. Like a parasite, it tries to take up space where it has no legal rights. It is not a resident—it is an intruder.

3. Your authority is your weapon. Battles are fought and won in the spirit, and your words carry the power to evict sickness. Just as Jesus rebuked fevers (**Luke 4:39**) and cast out spirits with a word (**Matthew 8:16**), you do the same:

"Disease, be gone in the name of Jesus!"

The moment you recognize **who you are in Christ**, Satan does too. He can no longer ask, *"Who are you?"* because he already knows—you carry the name of Jesus.

And when you do speak with authority? He does not negotiate. He obeys.

The Power of the Blood

When Jesus healed, He showed that **nothing is too big for God**—not sickness, not pain, not even death. The same Jesus who walked the earth healing the sick now lives inside of us.

The truth of **Isaiah 53** calls us to live differently. Jesus did not just save us from sin—He also gave us healing and authority. You can walk in this truth by declaring it over your life:

I am healed because of Jesus.
I have His authority to overcome sickness.
I live in God's grace every day.

When you embrace this truth, you can walk in confidence, knowing that healing and freedom are *ours* through Jesus. You are not striving to obtain them—they have been given. Understanding this makes it easier to live in bold faith, fully assured of what He has done. This is what it means to **rightly divide the Word**—to know the difference between what was promised and what has already been fulfilled. Jesus has *already* done it.

What would change in *your life* if you stopped striving and started possessing?

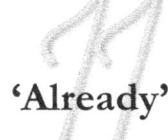

'Already'

As a believer, it is crucial to understand the authority you have in Christ. People can spend their lives reading and quoting scripture, which is good, but reading alone is not enough. It is like drinking water all day expecting to be fed—you will stay hydrated, but you will not be nourished. Similarly, quoting scripture without the power and authority of the Holy Spirit behind it is empty. It is like Paul said in 1 **Corinthians 2:1-5**:

"And I, brethren, when I came to you, came not with excellency of speech or of wisdom, declaring unto you the testimony of God. **For I determined not to know any thing among you, save Jesus Christ***, and him crucified. And I was with you in weakness, and in fear, and in much trembling. And my speech and my preaching was not with enticing words of man's wisdom,* **but in demonstration of the Spirit and of power: That your faith should not stand in the wisdom of men, but in the power of God.**"

Power comes not from intellectual knowledge or eloquent speech but from the Holy Spirit working in and through you.

Acts 19:15 bears repeating—the enemy recognizes genuine authority. If you do not truly know Jesus or understand the authority that resides in you, you cannot fully walk in what He has already provided.

The Sons of Sceva were like the Pharisees—both emphasized religious practices and traditions but lacked a genuine relationship with God. They relied on outward actions, but they did not possess the power that comes from dying to the flesh and making Jesus Lord overall.

As believers, this serves as a powerful reminder that **your authority comes not from what you do, but from who you are in Christ and the relationship you have with Him through the Holy Spirit.**

Unlocking the Door That is Already Open

Paul's words in **Galatians 4:16**— *'Am I therefore become your enemy, because I tell you the truth?'* reminds us that truth is often challenging, yet absolutely necessary. Sometimes, righteous anger is needed—not directed at God or others, but at Satan and the lies he uses to keep people in bondage. One of his greatest deceptions is convincing believers they must strive to earn righteousness by keeping the law, as if they are still under it.

If Satan can keep believers focused on *doing* instead of resting in what Christ has already done, he will trap them in cycles of bondage, depression, and desperate prayers. His goal is to exhaust believers, keeping them busy with performance-based Christianity—doing all the *'right'* things for Christ while missing the freedom found in Him. This often leads to burnout, resentment, and complacency. Even well-meaning affirmations like *'Good job'* can feel hollow when you are running on empty. Over time, you may find yourself doing more but feeling more distant from God, wondering, *what is the point?*

I have always enjoyed serving in different ways—it is in my nature to help and be involved. I simply love to *do*. But looking back, I see how the demands of serving so many people in various ways began to overwhelm me. At some point, I had to learn to say, *I am not able at this time.* That was one of the hardest lessons for me because I had grown accustomed to being part of every activity and event.

When I started pulling back, I imagine some people thought I had vanished for a while. But that was not the case. My decision to step away was intentional—a purposeful distancing so I could devote myself to studying God's Word and pursuing His calling. This shift was difficult because people often take offense when you do not attend events or are not as involved as you once were. But I knew I could not keep up that pace and fulfill God's calling on my life.

It was during this time of focused study and surrender that I was able to complete this book. Writing this book was one of my callings, and I realize now that stepping back was necessary to obey God and accomplish what He had placed in my heart to do. In this process, I gained a deeper revelation of the New Covenant and what it truly means for believers today.

When a believer understands the New Covenant, they realize that Jesus has already fulfilled the law and now lives within them. The Holy Spirit empowers them to live in a way that naturally fulfills the law—not through their own efforts, but through faith and love. As **Romans 8:3-4** says:

"For what the <u>law</u> could not do, in that it was <u>weak through the flesh</u>, God sending his own Son in the likeness of sinful flesh, and for sin, <u>condemned sin in the flesh</u>: That the righteousness of the law might be fulfilled in us, who walk not after the flesh, but after the Spirit."

There are two ways to approach teaching people about life in Christ.

1. You can teach them that their relationship with God is based on their own efforts—doing the right things, meeting certain standards, and believing that if they *'do what they are supposed to,'* then God will respond with favor. But this only leads to frustration and striving because it puts the burden on them to <u>earn</u> His blessings, rather than receiving what He has already provided.
2. Or you can teach them to place their faith in the finished work of Christ. This shifts the focus from *what they must do* to *what Christ has already done.* When they trust Him, His Spirit works through them, guiding their actions and transforming their lives in a way that naturally reflects His character. It is **not** about abandoning good works but about changing the motivation behind them. Instead of striving for God's approval, their actions flow from gratitude and a deep relationship with Him.

Jesus said in **Matthew 5:48**, *"Be ye therefore perfect, even as your Father which is in heaven is perfect."*

This does not mean striving for human perfection—it is about spiritual maturity. As you trust God, the Holy Spirit transforms us into His image. True maturity is not about trying harder—it is about surrendering to His work in us. The more you trust, the more you reflect His nature, not by effort, but by *grace.*

What God Has Already Done

When you shift your focus from striving to simply believing, peace takes over. You begin to extend grace to others, no longer holding them to your own standards, because you recognize that God has accomplished everything necessary. *It is finished*. His work is complete, and He has **already** provided:

- **He has already answered your prayers:** *"And this is the confidence that we have in him, that, if we ask any thing according to his will, he heareth us: And if we know that he hear us, whatsoever we ask, we know that we have the petitions that we desired of him."* (**1 John 5:14-15**)

- **He has already healed you:**
"Who his own self bare our sins in his own body on the tree, that we, being dead to sins, should live unto righteousness: by whose stripes ye were healed." (**1 Peter 2:24**)

-**He has already equipped you to heal others:** *"Verily, verily, I say unto you, He that believeth on me, the works that I do shall he do also; and greater works than these shall he do; because I go unto my Father."* (**John 14:12**)

- **He has already provided for you:**
"But my God shall supply all your need according to his riches in glory by Christ Jesus." (**Philippians 4:19**)

- **He has already given you peace:**
"Peace I leave with you, my peace I give unto you: not as the world giveth, give I unto you. Let not your heart be troubled, neither let it be afraid." (**John 14:27**)

- **He has already given you victory:**
"But thanks be to God, which giveth us the victory through our Lord Jesus Christ." (**1 Corinthians 15:57**)

- **He has already delivered you from darkness:**
"Who hath <u>delivered</u> us from the power of darkness, and hath translated us into the kingdom of his dear Son." (**Colossians 1:13**)

- **He has already redeemed you:**
"In whom we <u>have</u> redemption through his blood, the <u>forgiveness</u> of sins, according to the riches of his grace." (**Ephesians 1:7**)

- **He has already made a way for you:**
"Thus saith the LORD, which <u>maketh a way</u> in the sea, and a path in the mighty waters." (**Isaiah 43:16**)

- **He has already blessed you with all spiritual blessings:**
"<u>Blessed</u> be the God and Father of our Lord Jesus Christ, who hath blessed us with all spiritual blessings in heavenly places in Christ." (**Ephesians 1:3**)

- **He has already defeated your enemies:**
"The LORD shall cause thine enemies that rise up against thee to be <u>smitten</u> before thy face: they shall come out against thee one way, <u>and flee</u> before thee seven ways." (**Deuteronomy 28:7**)

- **He has already made you more than a conqueror:**
"Nay, in all these things we <u>are</u> more than conquerors through him that loved us." (**Romans 8:37**)

- **He has already overcome the world for you:**
"These things I have spoken unto you, that in me ye might have peace. In the world ye shall have tribulation: but be of good cheer; I <u>have</u> overcome the world." (**John 16:33**)

- **He has already given you victory over sin and death:**
"For sin shall <u>not</u> have dominion over you: for ye are <u>not</u> <u>under</u> <u>the</u> <u>law</u>, but <u>under grace</u>." (**Romans 6:14**)

- **He has already forgiven you:**
*"And you, <u>being</u> <u>dead</u> <u>in</u> <u>your</u> sins and the uncircumcision of your flesh, hath he quickened together with him, having <u>forgiven you</u> **all** trespasses."* (**Colossians 2:13**)

- **He has already made you righteous:**
"For he <u>hath</u> <u>made</u> him to be sin for us, who knew no sin; that we might be made the righteousness of God in him." (**2 Corinthians 5:21**)

- **He has already given you power over the enemy:**
"Ye are of God, little children, and <u>have</u> <u>overcome</u> them: because greater is he that is in you, than he that is in the world." (**1 John 4:4**)

- **He has already given you the power to triumph in every situation:**
"Now thanks be unto God, which <u>always</u> causeth us to triumph in Christ, and maketh manifest the savour of his knowledge by us in every place." (**2 Corinthians 2:14**)

- **He has already given you the armor to stand against the enemy:**
"Finally, my brethren, be strong in the Lord, and in the power of his might. Put on the whole armour of God, that ye may be able to <u>stand</u> against the wiles of the devil." (**Ephesians 6:10-11**)

- **He has already made you victorious through faith:**
"For whatsoever is born of God <u>overcometh the world</u>: and this <u>is</u> the victory that overcometh the world, even our faith." (**1 John 5:4**)

This list is more than a reminder; it is a declaration of the totality of Christ's finished work. Everything needed for life and godliness has **already** been provided through Him. Our role is to walk in faith, embracing what He has accomplished, and to live with the confidence and freedom His grace has secured. Let this truth renew your mind and empower you to live boldly as a testimony of His victory.

Simple, Yet Powerful

You have the power living inside you. You *only* must believe it. It really is that simple. As **Psalms 119:130** says: *"The entrance of thy words giveth light; it giveth understanding unto the simple."*

God's Word was never meant to be complicated or burdensome. It brings clarity, wisdom, and guidance to those who seek it. Jesus said:

Matthew 11:25:
"I thank thee, O Father, Lord of heaven and earth, because thou hast hid these things from the wise and prudent, and hast revealed them unto babes."

2 Corinthians 11:3:
"But I fear, lest by any means, as the serpent beguiled Eve through his subtilty, so your minds should be corrupted from the <u>simplicity</u> that is in Christ."

- This verse emphasizes the simplicity of Christ and warns against **overcomplicating** or corrupting **the truth.**

God's Word becomes clear and powerful when you approach it with humility, seeking His **truth** rather than relying on our own knowledge. It is not about overcomplicating things or blindly accepting what others say. It is about seeking truth for yourself—letting the Holy Spirit reveal it to you in a way that transforms your life.

Restoring Faith-Based Prayer

Moving Beyond Pleading Prayers

For years, I prayed like most people do—pleading, asking, and hoping. But the more I begged, the less I believed. My prayers were filled with uncertainty, not confidence. My words were desperate, not expectant. I thought I needed to **convince** God to act, but here is what I did not realize: He had already answered.

Prayer is not about convincing God—it is about aligning my heart with what He has already spoken.

Faith does not beg. Faith receives.

At the time, I thought my prayers were strong. They sounded spiritual—full of flowery phrases and repetitions I had heard my whole life. I would say, *"Lord, I thank You, Father, for who You are, and I ask You to continue to lead, guide, and direct our steps..."* as if He were suddenly going to stop doing those things. I thought the more I prayed, the more powerful my words would become.

But Jesus warned against this kind of empty, repetitive prayer.

Matthew 6:5-7—Jesus' Warning Against Hypocritical Prayer

"And when thou prayest, thou shalt not be as the hypocrites are: for they love to pray standing in the synagogues and in the corners of the streets, that they may be seen of men. Verily I say unto you, They have their reward."
"But thou, when thou prayest, enter into thy closet, and when thou hast shut thy door, pray to thy Father which is in secret; and thy Father which seeth in

secret shall reward thee openly."
"<u>But when ye pray, use not vain repetitions</u>, as the heathen do: for they think that they shall be heard for their much speaking."

Jesus exposed prayer that relied on performance instead of relationship. He was not condemning long prayers—He was condemning prayers without faith.

That is exactly what I had been doing. My prayers were filled with vain repetition—words spoken out of habit, not belief. I thought my words would move God, but God is not moved by desperate words—He is moved by faith.

God says, *"My people are destroyed for lack of knowledge"* (**Hosea 4:6**).

Plain and simple, I was ignorant of His Word. I misunderstood most of the scriptures I read because I did not grasp how to read them in context. The rest of my understanding came from traditions, not from true revelation.

But the moment I shifted from rehearsed begging to believing, everything fell into place.

That is what this chapter is about—restoring faith-based prayer and letting go of the habit of pleading.

Healing Through Faith, Not Pleading

Have you ever noticed that the New Testament never instructs us to pray and ask God to heal? Think about that.

While Scripture emphasizes prayer, faith, and seeking God, it does so from a position of believing that healing has already been provided through Jesus' finished work on the cross. *You are not trying to get healed*—you are enforcing the healing that is already yours. The work is done; the only question is whether you will believe it or keep waiting for proof.

In **James 5:14-15**, we read:

"Is any sick among you? let him call for the elders of the church; and let them pray over him, anointing him with oil in the name of the Lord: And the prayer of faith shall save the sick, and the Lord shall raise him up; and if he have committed sins, they shall be forgiven him."

This passage highlights the prayer of faith—not pleading or uncertainty, but confident trust in God's provision. Two key points stand out:

1. Calling the Elders – This reflects the importance of mature believers—those grounded in faith and wisdom who understand God's promises and can pray with unwavering confidence. Those who are called to pray over others must have a revelation of grace.

    An elder, in the biblical sense, is not just someone with a title, but someone mature in faith—one who rightly divides the Word and walks in the fullness of what Christ has accomplished. If they are still operating under the law, their prayers will lack the authority that comes from standing in Christ's finished work.

    This is something to consider: Would you rather receive prayer from someone walking in the freedom of grace or from someone still striving under the weight of the law? This aligns with **2 Timothy 2:15**, which calls believers to rightly divide the Word of Truth.

2. The Role of Faith in Prayer – The *prayer of faith* is the responsibility of the one leading the prayer. Nowhere does Scripture suggest that healing only happens if the sick person has enough faith.

The Role of the One Leading the Prayer

A common misconception is that healing only happens if the person being prayed for has enough faith. This idea shifts the burden of faith from the one leading the prayer to the one receiving it. But if that were true, then whose faith raised Lazarus from the dead? He was dead—he could not exercise *enough* faith for himself! Clearly, it was Jesus' faith in the Father's power that resulted in Lazarus rising from the grave (**John 11:41-43**):

"Then they took away the stone from the place where the dead was laid. And Jesus lifted up his eyes, and said, Father, I thank thee that thou <u>hast heard</u> me. And I knew that thou hearest me always: but because of the people which stand by I said it, that they may believe that thou hast sent me."

Notice how Jesus thanked God **before** Lazarus even came forth. Jesus knew that God heard Him, and He prayed with unwavering faith. It was not Lazarus' faith but Jesus' faith in the Father's power that brought about the miracle.

This is what faith-based prayer looks like.

Faith-Based Prayer in Action

The moment you stop begging and start believing:
- You pray differently.
- You speak differently.
- You expect differently.

You no longer approach God like a distant ruler who might say no—You approach Him like a Father who has already said yes.

And that is when it clicked. My prayers were no longer about sounding right—they were about standing in truth.

- I no longer begged for healing—I declared, *"By His stripes, I am healed."* (**Isaiah 53:5**)
- I no longer pleaded for peace—I rested in, *"My peace I give unto you."* (**John 14:27**)
- I no longer asked for strength—I stood on, *"I can do all things through Christ."* (**Philippians 4:13**)

And I saw the results —not because I was waiting for proof, but because faith naturally produces fruit. My prayers were no longer about hoping something would change; they were about standing in the truth that it already had.

Prayers were no longer just words—they became declarations backed by faith.

If prayer feels like a struggle, ask yourself:
Am I praying with faith, or am I pleading out of doubt?

Faith-filled prayer is not about getting God's attention—it is about stepping into what He has already made available.

Conclusion: Praying From Victory, Not for Victory

Faith-based prayer is not about asking God to move—it is about standing on the fact that He already has.

When you pray with this certainty, everything shifts.

Let this truth sink in:
- God has already said yes.
- The answer has already been given.
- The breakthrough has already been provided.

You do not have to beg God to do what He has already promised.

You pray from victory—not for victory.

Stop pleading. Start believing. It is finished.

Stop Chasing a Dollar

Breaking Free from the Cycle

There were so many times our bank account over the years had reached an all-time low—really low. Oftentimes my husband was out of work because of the type of work he did. Bills kept piling up, and it felt like we were drowning in debt all over again. This cycle had gone on for years.

The problem was not a lack of effort or determination—it was the belief that we always had to do more to earn more, constantly searching for extra income. We were raised with a strong work ethic, and in our limited understanding, is how we survived all these years. We thought we were working smarter, not harder, but that could not have been further from the truth. There is nothing wrong with hard work, but when it consumes your thought process to the point that your bank account becomes a burden, things are out of balance. Plain and simple.

No matter who was working, where they were working, or what was happening, we could never seem to make ends meet. Over the years, I have studied life-changing books on finances and provision. Though they deeply impacted me *at the time,* somehow, we always ended up back in the same financial struggle a few months later. (I had not yet fully understood grace). This appeared to be our normal for years. My understanding of why I kept falling back into this mindset did not come to full fruition until later.

I always attributed our setbacks to either his health concerns or lack of work, saying to myself, *'Well, we got started late in life.'* That was not it, nor was it the fact that I was not receiving breakthroughs from the lessons I had studied. It did not matter how much was in our account—my mind was more focused on what I needed to keep doing to ensure our future.

Satan never stops attacking the mind. But the truth is, the more we chased the dollar, the further it ran from us. That is when I realized—the issue was not just our finances. It was our thinking. The real battle was not just about money; it was about how we viewed provision itself.

The Mindset Trap

Shifting your mindset does not usually happen overnight. People are deeply rooted in what they believe, and even when they see that their way is not working, they often keep doing the same thing because it is all they have ever known or just the way they were raised.

It is not that they do not want change—it is that they do not know how to change. You can see this everywhere—people grind themselves into exhaustion, stress about bills, and live paycheck to paycheck, believing this is just how life works. It is normal for them, even if it is painful. And Satan knows this. He knows that if he can keep people locked into a scarcity mindset, they will never step into God's provision.

That is why Scripture constantly warns against being bound by tradition. The New Testament repeatedly emphasizes this— teaching believers how to move beyond a mindset of striving and step into God's way of doing things. The financial struggle is not just about money—it is about learning to operate under Kingdom principles instead of earthly effort. Yet, just as in Jesus' day, some will struggle to see it just like we failed to.

In Matthew, Jesus explains that some simply will not get it—not because the truth is not available, but because their hearts are not ready to receive it. This is not a matter of intelligence; it is a matter of the spiritual condition of the heart. A lot of believers hear it, but few truly grasp it, because they are filtering it through what they have always known.

Jesus came to break us free from this kind of endless striving. That is why the New Testament focuses so much on renewing the mind—because until people see things differently, they will continue to live the same way.

It is important to recognize Jesus did not just perform miracles—He taught.

He knew that unless people changed how they thought, they would go right back to their old ways. Healing the sick, casting out demons, and forgiving sins was only part of the work—the bigger mission was to open people's eyes to the truth. And the reality is, God never intended for His people to chase money or live a life of strife.

It was always meant to flow freely to those who seek Him first.

Stepping Into God's Plan

For years, my husband and I talked about getting our contractor's license. It was always at the back of our minds, but with his nonstop work schedule, there was never time to pursue it. He poured himself into providing for our family, and I saw the weight of that responsibility on his shoulders. I wanted to do something to help—something that would not just lighten the load but also position our business for greater opportunities. Then, God placed a desire in my heart to go after the license myself. It was more than what I thought to be just a promising idea—it was a calling. I knew this was not just about me; it was about stepping into something bigger than I could see at the time. So, I made a decision: if he was not able to step away long enough to go for it, then I would. I would take on the challenge, study, and do what needed to be done to move us forward. I had no idea the road ahead would test my faith in ways I never expected. But one thing I did know—when God plants a vision in your heart, He also provides the strength to see it through.

Stepping out in faith does not mean the journey will be easy. Looking back, it felt like a season in the wilderness—where God was preparing doors to open long before I could see them. He had placed a vision in my heart, but at the time, it was still unclear. And just when I took that step of faith, life hit hard. One challenge after another came crashing in, each one testing my resolve. But even in the struggle, God's hand was undeniable—strengthening me, sustaining me, and reminding me why I started in the first place.

These were some of the obstacles that could have stopped me—but instead, they became part of my testimony:

- In 2020, the pandemic turned the world upside down—and ours was no exception. My husband was laid off, and overnight, our steady income was gone.
- With no financial safety net, we had to figure things out fast. The only money coming in was my small check, which barely covered the essentials. But the Lord opened a door we never expected—tree removal. What started as a desperate attempt to make ends meet turned into a lucrative business, sustaining us in a time when many were struggling.
- But even in survival mode, something stirred inside me. I could not shake the desire to pass the general contractor's exam. It made no sense at the time—our focus was on making ends meet—but the dream would not let go of me.
- So, I started small. One book, then another. Each purchase felt like a step of faith, even though I had no idea how or when I would be able to get the rest.

- Then, the bottom fell out—or so I thought at the time. My husband was diagnosed with liver cancer. After surgery, he was fighting to regain his strength while the economy was still struggling. He ended up being out of work for five months.
- What Satan intended for harm became the very thing that led me into a deeper understanding of Spiritual Authority. What felt like a season of complete loss was actually the beginning of a revelation—one that would change everything.
- He could not even lift a chainsaw—but God's hand was still at work. Even in the uncertainty, we never went without.

I put the exam on hold. Life was overwhelming, and I was just trying to hold everything together.

But the vision never left me.

Mark eventually made a full recovery and went back to work. By 2023, I had purchased all twenty-three books. And by this time, I was not just going for a NC general contractor's license—I made up my mind to pursue NASCLA certification, which would allow me to take licensing exams in sixteen states.

I knew I could not achieve this on my own.

And just when I thought the weight could not get any heavier, my mama had a stroke.

For a while, everything else faded into the background. Nothing mattered more than being there for her. My goals, my plans—even my studying—were put on hold as I stepped into the role of caretaker.

A Mother's Faith & God's Strength

I took six months off from work to care for her. During that time, I slowly resumed studying. At first, it felt impossible, but then something unexpected happened—Mama became part of the process. I let her call out test questions for me, and it gave her something to be involved in. It was slow, but it was ours. We laughed through it, even in the midst of everything. As time went on, I returned to work full-time while continuing to care for Mama, balancing long days of studying and helping my husband with tree removal. It was exhausting, but I kept pushing forward.

Then, on the day I was supposed to take my test, Mama had an appointment to get her lung test results. My sister had called to say she was sick and unable to go so without hesitation, I rescheduled my exam.

That is when we got the news: stage 4 cancer.

But that diagnosis never took hold in her mind, and we did not let it take hold in ours.
I reminded her of what God had spoken to me when she first had the stroke:
"Whose report are you going to believe?"
We prayed and believed she was healed.
With unwavering faith, she told the doctors, *"I am not going home to die. I am going home to live."* That day, as we sat in the parking lot of the doctor's office, she turned to me and said, *"Lee, I want to live to see Cainan graduate."*

And live she did.

She went to every one of my son's games unless she had an appointment.
She showed up at every function she could.
She followed my niece and her daughter to all her events.

She kept my sister and me busy, taking her everywhere she wanted to go.

She embraced life.

It was during this time that I passed the General Contractors exam and earned my license. But as time went on, Mama grew weary. One day, she sat my sister and me down and told us plainly —it was nearing her time to go *'home.'*

One week after my boy graduated high school, on Father's Day of that year, she went home to be with the Lord.

Looking back, it was God who sustained me through that season—working two jobs, caring for Mama, and pursuing this dream. And through it all, grace was already transforming my understanding, but I had yet to fully grasp what it meant to live by grace. I had studied it, I had spoken about it, but now, I had to walk it out.

That was when I learned something that changed my life: *The same way my mother refused to let a diagnosis define her life, I had to refuse to let my circumstances define mine.*

She walked in faith, not fear. And if I truly trusted God's provision, I had to do the same. Provision is not something you strive for—it is something you trust in. And because she lived by faith, not fear, she truly lived.

A God-Given Vision Strengthens Faith

Here is the key:

When God places a vision in your heart, it is meant to grow you and teach you to depend on Him and His provision.

Chasing a dollar, on the other hand, happens when you stop relying on Him and start leaning on your own strength.

One thing is certain:
If He gave you the vision, He will give you the provision.
If He planted the desire, He will plant the resources.

That is why chasing money is the wrong mindset—money follows faith, not the other way around.

Let the Dollar Chase You

During a training later that year, I met a woman who owned several successful businesses.

I asked her, *"What's the one takeaway you've gained from all your accomplishments?"*

She smiled and said, *"Never chase the dollar—let it chase you."*

That one statement hit me like a revelation. It aligned with everything God had been speaking to me over the past year.

But that did not mean the challenges stopped. If anything, the attacks on our finances only intensified. The enemy will always try to shake your confidence—especially when you begin walking in God's provision.

What is the Enemy Really After?

Jesus gives us the answer in **John 10:10**: *"The thief cometh not, but for to steal, and to kill, and to destroy: I am come that they might have life, and that they might have it more abundantly."*

Satan's real goal is to steal the Word planted in your heart—not just your paycheck. When Jesus says the thief comes to *steal, kill, and destroy*, it aligns with **Matthew 13:19**, where Jesus explains the parable of the sower:

"When any one heareth the word of the kingdom, and understandeth it not, then cometh the wicked one, and catcheth away that which was sown in his heart."

This verse reveals Satan's primary strategy—to steal the truth before it can take root. The enemy is not just after your money, health, or circumstances. His real target is the Word of God in your heart because that Word has the power to produce faith, renew your mind, and transform your life.

But notice the key part—*"and understandeth it not."* Jesus makes it clear that when someone does not fully grasp the Word, it becomes vulnerable to being stolen. This is not just about ignorance, but about a lack of revelation. The Greek word for understand (suniemi) means to grasp, perceive, or put together the meaning of something—not just hearing words, but truly connecting with their significance.

If the enemy can keep you from understanding—if he can keep you focused on religious performance, doubt, or distraction—then he can keep you from walking in the abundant life Jesus came to give. Many believers hear the Word but never truly comprehend what Christ has already provided. They may:

- View salvation as just a religious ritual instead of a transformation.
- See healing as a possibility rather than a finished work.
- Think grace must be earned instead of received freely.

Without understanding, faith cannot grow (**Romans 10:17**). And when faith does not grow, people remain stuck in cycles of lack, frustration, and striving.

That is why it is so important to stay rooted in truth and renew your mind daily. The moment you stop chasing the dollar and start pursuing the truth of God's Word, you position yourself to receive His abundant blessings. Instead of praying for breakthroughs, you start walking in the fullness of what Christ already provided.

The Power of True Provision

There is a difference between chasing money and walking in provision. When you chase money, you are always striving—always working harder, worrying more, and feeling like there is never enough. But when you trust God as your source, money follows you.

We came to understand this in a season that tested everything we believed about God's provision. There was a time when everything seemed to be drying up. Jobs were inconsistent, bills were stacking up, and the temptation to panic was real. We had seen God provide before, but this time, the pressure felt heavier. Every logical thought said, *'You need to hustle harder, find another way, make something happen."* But instead of running in fear, we chose to stand on what we knew to be true: *God is our provider.*

Then, without us striving, doors began to open. Work came—not in a trickle, but in a flood. Contracts we had been waiting on for months were suddenly approved. Jobs we had not even pursued were offered to us. It was as if provision had been waiting for us to step into trust before it could be released.

That is when it clicked: Provision was never something we had to chase. It was something we had to walk in.

The world teaches that financial security comes through grinding, hustling, and doing whatever it takes to get ahead. But the kingdom of God operates differently. *Seek first the kingdom of God, and all these things shall be added unto you* (**Matthew 6:33**). That does not mean sit back and do nothing—it means align your heart with God's Word, work with integrity, and trust that the blessing follows obedience.

When you truly understand this, money no longer controls you—you control it. You stop chasing it, and it starts chasing you. Because in God's kingdom, provision is not earned. It is released through faith.

Provision is not a one-time event—it is a continual walk of faith. Just as seasons change, so do financial flows. And when it feels like resources are drying up, that is when faith is truly tested.

What Happens When Provision Tapers Off?

What happens when the floodgates seem to close? When the provision that once poured in suddenly slows to a trickle?

This is where many people start to **doubt**, wondering, *Did I do something wrong?* or *Is God withholding?* But just like seasons change, provision has seasons too.

When work slows down, when the finances feel tight again, it is not a sign that God has abandoned you—it is a reminder to stay rooted in trust, not fear.

God never called us to live from one financial high to the next, constantly riding the waves of abundance and drought. He called us to walk by faith, not by sight (**2 Corinthians 5:7**). That means whether the provision is overflowing or seemingly scarce, our confidence remains the same:

- God is still our provider.
- We are still walking in His blessing.
- We are not chasing money—it is following us.

Seasons of plenty test our stewardship, and seasons of scarcity test our trust. But neither defines our security—God does.

So, when provision seems to taper off, it is not a sign to panic—it is a call to stand firm. The real question is not, *"Did I do something wrong?"* but rather, *"Will I keep trusting the One who has never failed me?"*

Replacing Lies

The Battle for Your Mind

Spiritual warfare is constant, and the enemy does not wait until you are ready. The battle for your mind is fought daily—through thoughts, fears, and the lies whispered to your heart. Every day, in every situation, you face opportunities to either stand firm in God's Word or allow the enemy to gain ground.

The enemy's greatest weapon is deception—if he can make you believe a lie, your actions will follow. This became clear to me one night when a dream exposed a battle I had not realized I was in.

Exposing the Deeper Battle

Recently, I had a conversation with someone whose mother was struggling with difficult life choices. The weight of that conversation stayed with me. Challenges, especially those faced by the people we love, aren't just physical or emotional—they are spiritual battles. I knew this and had been studying my Word that morning, but instead of countering that burden with the Word of God, I let it settle in my mind.

That night, I had a dream.

I have had dreams of demonic possession for years. In the past, I was always on the defensive—struggling to mutter the name of Jesus, feeling powerless and barely able to resist. But over time, I learned how to fight back.

Through David Hernandez's teaching, I gained a deeper understanding that spiritual authority requires confronting the enemy head-on, not backing down. When I applied that truth, the dreams became rare. And when they did come, I now **stepped toward** the demon, and the dream would fade. It is the same in life—when faced with fear, you do not turn away; you step toward it with the knowledge of who you are in Christ. This truth illuminated the power of Scripture in my life:

Joshua 1:9 – *"Have I not <u>commanded</u> you? Be strong and of good courage; do not be afraid, nor be dismayed, for the Lord your God is with you wherever you go."*

I finally understood I have authority over Satan. But that night, something was different. In the dream, I stood in front of a mirror and felt a demonic presence trying to possess me. A sudden fear crept in. I knew my guard was down, as if I had returned to a place of powerlessness. I tried to call on Jesus, but my words lacked authority. I felt paralyzed. My spirit knew what to do, but my mind was not ready.

Desperate, I looked around and spotted my son. I turned to him for prayer, hoping he could help. He had been learning about spiritual authority, but his understanding was still growing. I reached out, but something felt off—his reaction was hesitant, uncertain.

I searched for others, but they did not recognize the battle I was in. No one seemed to understand what was happening or even acknowledge it.

I felt powerless. Then I saw my reflection again. My right cheek dropped. *'I'm having a stroke,'* I thought. But at that moment, something snapped inside me. *'No. That is a lie.'* I denounced it, and instantly, the illusion shattered. I woke up to my husband shaking me, saying I was having a nightmare.

That dream was not just a warning—it was a revelation.

The Lesson God Revealed

God showed me immediately—this was a spiritual battle, and I had allowed the enemy's lies to settle in my mind instead of replacing them with truth. It was not the conversation that had opened the door—it was my response.

It is a commitment. Renewing your mind (**Romans 12:2**) is not a one-time event—it is a daily commitment. It means aligning your thoughts with His Word in every situation. Without realizing it, I briefly slipped back into trusting in my own strength. It hit me like lightning. This dream was not about fear—it was a reminder to stay armed. It was a lesson in replacing every lie, fear, and emotional burden with the truth of Scripture.

To be clear, Scripture does not call us to walk around all day holding a Bible—it calls us to carry His Word in our hearts. That is the difference.

Why Replacing Lies with the Word Is Vital

The enemy thrives on deception. He does not need to overpower you—he only needs you to believe a lie. Fear, doubt, and insecurity are his tools, and he waits to see if you will accept them.

But as a believer, you have the authority to shut him down—if you respond with the Word of God. When fear or doubt creep in, pause and ask yourself:
"What is the enemy trying to make me believe?"

Once you recognize the lie, replace it immediately with truth. Scripture is your weapon, sharper than any two-edged sword (**Hebrews 4:12**). Do not just think about it—speak it.

The Word is not just for defense—it is for offense.

A Call to Spiritual Readiness

This chapter serves as a reminder for all of us: Spiritual warfare is real, and the enemy's attacks are relentless. As believers, you are **not** a victim—you **are** victorious. The key is staying rooted in God's Word. The Word is not a shield you pick up only when you are under attack—it is a sword you carry at all times. When the enemy attacks, do not back down— step forward. Speak the Word.

Declare the truth. Watch the lies crumble. Victory is not something you wait for—it is something you walk in daily.

Attacking the Root, Not the Fruit

Fighting the Right Battle

When someone falls back into sin, it is easy to focus on what you can see—their actions, their decisions, the changes in their behavior. People start asking questions like:

"Why did they go back to that habit?"
"When did they stop going to church?"
"What caused this?"

But those questions miss the real issue. By the time you notice the outward signs of backsliding, the enemy has already been working beneath the surface.

Too often, people focus on the fruit when the real battle is actually at the root.

Here is what you need to understand: behavior is just a symptom—the *root issue* is *spiritual*.

If you only react to what you see, you are already too late.

Outward Signs Are the Result, Not the Cause

When someone begins to backslide, it can often become evident through external changes like:

- Avoiding family and friends
- Skipping church services

- Speaking negatively or acting out of character
- Returning to destructive habits they once left behind.

But these outward changes are just smoke—they are not the fire itself.

The real battle was already lost in their mind. If you only react to behavior, it is like fixing a crack in the wall without repairing the foundation.

As believers, look deeper. Focus on the main objective, immediately speaking life over them and declaring they are still who God says they are. Remind them of God's love, His promises, and the identity He has given them. Instead of reinforcing their failures, speak the truth—**They are redeemed, loved, and never beyond His reach.**

When you see someone drifting, respond with restoration. **Galatians 6:1** reminds us: *"Brethren, if a man is overtaken in any trespass, you who are spiritual restore such a one in a spirit of gentleness, considering yourself lest you also be tempted."*

The Spiritual Battle Comes First

Ephesians 6:12 reminds us:

"For we wrestle not against flesh and blood, but against principalities, against powers, against the rulers of the darkness of this world, against spiritual wickedness in high places."

By the time someone starts pulling away from God, the battle has already taken place in the unseen realm.

The enemy gains access through:

- **Distraction** – Busyness, entertainment, and worldly concerns shift their focus away from God. Their priorities become misaligned.
- **Deception** – Small lies take root and grow. What starts as a simple compromise or unchecked thought can lead to a complete stronghold.

- **Separation** – Isolation makes the enemy's whispers louder. He loves to pull people away from relationships that strengthen them.
- **Discouragement** – Shame, doubt, and feelings of failure make them question their worth, God's love, or whether they can ever change.

These attacks begin long before you see the outward signs appear. That is why you must fight the battle at the source. If you only focus on outward behavior, you miss the deeper issue—the state of the heart and mind.

Jesus made this clear in **Matthew 12:43-45** when He warned about the danger of spiritual emptiness:

"When an unclean spirit goes out of a man, he goes through dry places, seeking rest, and finds none. Then he says, 'I will return to my house from which I came.' And when he comes, he finds it empty, swept, and put in order. Then he goes and takes with him seven other spirits more wicked than himself, and they enter and dwell there; and the last state of that man is worse than the first. So shall it also be with this wicked generation."

At first glance, this passage seems to be about backsliding into sin—but it actually reveals something much deeper: it is possible to appear *'clean'* on the outside while remaining spiritually empty on the inside.

This is where believers get caught. They measure their spiritual health by how well they are performing rather than whether they are truly being transformed. They think as long as they are doing all they can, staying away from *'major'* sins, and keeping their lives in order, they are fine. But Jesus was not only referring to those who fall into blatant rebellion—He was warning those who think an outwardly put-together life means they are spiritually secure.

The deception is subtle. A person can *'clean up'* their life yet remain completely exposed to the enemy because they have not been <u>filled with God's **truth**</u>. That is why **Galatians 6:1** reminds us that anyone can be tempted. The enemy does not need someone to reject God outright—he just needs them to rely on their own efforts instead of true spiritual renewal.

Paul makes this clear in **Romans 12:2**: A renewed mind is a protected mind. If you stay filled with God's Word, you do not just avoid backsliding—you guard against the slow drift into self-reliance, spiritual complacency, and performance-based faith. This is the real danger Jesus was exposing: a person who believes they are standing firm while unknowingly making themselves an easy target.

Why Striving Falls Short

When you see a loved one backsliding, our natural response is to try and *'fix'* it.

While this may come from a place of love, it rarely works—because you cannot fix a spiritual battle with human effort.

All that does is push them deeper into shame and frustration. I learned this firsthand.

When Love Is Not Enough

For years, my sister and I tried to help our daddy overcome what was labeled as alcohol addiction.

I never understood why love alone did not change things.

'Why can't he just look at us—his family—and stop?' *'Can't he see how much we love him?'*

I knew he cared about us. I knew he did not want to hurt us. But love, on its own, was not the solution—because the battle was not just physical.

It was spiritual.

No amount of begging, reasoning, or pushing could break the chains holding him.

Real, lasting change does not come from pressuring someone to change their actions. It comes from breaking the enemy's hold at the root. And while all prayer has power, it is prayer with authority—rooted in the finished work of Christ—that truly sets people free. It comes from breaking the enemy's hold at the root.

That is something only *prayer* with *authority* can do.

Stop Pleading—Start Commanding!

For years, I approached sickness, attacks, and spiritual battles like most people do—hoping for change, waiting for a breakthrough, just trying to *'get through it.'*

It felt like an endless cycle.

But then I learned what true authority in Christ means.

Now, when sickness tries to creep into my home, I shut the door in Satan's face.

When the enemy whispers lies into my mind, I shut him down with the Word.

When he tries to attack my family, he has picked the wrong house!

Because he has no authority here.

Isaiah 54:17 says:

"No weapon that is formed against thee shall prosper."

No weapon formed against Christ can prosper. And I am His child—so no weapon formed against me can prosper.

I believe that.

When I pray, I do not beg for victory.

I pray *from* victory.

Attacking the Root—True Freedom

So how do we actually attack the root?

It starts with shifting the focus from behavior to belief. If you only react to what you see—their actions, failures, or struggles—you are dealing with the fruit, not the root. But when you **speak** to who they truly are in Christ, **you plant** seeds of <u>truth</u> that challenge the lies keeping them bound.

Speak Life, Not Judgment

Proverbs 18:21 *tells us:*
"Death and life are in the power of the tongue."

What an incredible responsibility. Instead of saying:
"Look at the mess they made...."
"Why won't they just listen?"
"They always do this."
You could say (with conviction):
"You are deeply loved."
"God's plan for you hasn't changed."
"You are still His child, and He still calls you by name."

This may seem passive, but it is not! Speaking life, plants seeds of hope, even when they act like they are not listening.

This is not about ignoring sin or pretending things are fine. It is about recognizing that behavior only changes when beliefs do. If someone begins to see themselves through God's eyes—loved, forgiven, and empowered—that is when real transformation happens. Not because you forced it, but because you stopped reacting to the fruit and started speaking to the root.

The Transformative Power of Grace

Introduction: Grace Changes Everything

Grace is not just a doctrine—it is the foundation of the entire Christian life. From salvation to daily life, grace is the key to everything.

Paul preached grace with *passion* because he knew firsthand how it transforms. He had once been a man consumed by religious works, striving to earn righteousness by the law. But an encounter with Jesus changed him forever. He **discovered** that *righteousness* was **not** something to achieve—it was something to receive. And that revelation changed his life.

The same is true today. Pay close attention because this is where many believers struggle in their faith, not because they do not love God, but because they do not fully understand grace. They still strive, still carry guilt, still feel unworthy—because they have been established in a mindset of *doing* in order to get God to do. It is not about you or the works you do for Him. Paul realized this.

This chapter will walk through Paul's teachings on grace, showing how it saves, sustains, and strengthens every believer. If you have ever felt like you were not enough—not good enough, not strong enough, not faithful enough—or if your focus has been centered on what others do or do not do, then it is time to let grace change that.

1. Salvation: Grace as the Only Way to Be Saved

Many hesitate to come to God for different reasons. Some believe they must clean up their lives first, while others feel unworthy. Some fear they will have to give up everything they enjoy, and still others find salvation too complicated to grasp.

But Paul makes it clear that salvation is not something we **earn**—it is a **gift**.

Ephesians 2:8-9 says:
For by grace are ye saved through faith; and that not of yourselves: it is the gift of God: Not of works, lest any man should boast.

Salvation is not about human effort, rule-following, or striving to be better. It is about grace—God's undeserved favor—received by faith.

The Moment Grace Found Me

I was young when I first experienced a *"Sister Joyce Revival"* as we called it, in Shallotte, NC. I saw people moved by the Spirit, and though I did not fully understand it, I wanted in. My friends went up for prayer, so I followed. Looking back, I was so young that I do not even know if I truly got saved that day.

But years later, the experience was different.

I was sitting in church, and I could not be still. An overwhelming desire built inside me—something I could not ignore. It was more than emotion; it was a pulling, an undeniable calling to surrender my whole life to God.

I sat there, struggling—struggling with what others might think, struggling with what I might have to give up. All the hesitations that keep people from stepping into grace were running through my mind.

But the moment I gave in, the moment I surrendered to what could only be described as *His calling*, it was as if something physically lifted off my shoulders. I cried like a baby. A weight I did not even realize I was carrying was suddenly gone.

That was grace.

Salvation is not about figuring everything out or proving you are worthy—it is about responding to His call and receiving what has already been given.

2. You Get Saved. Now What?

Someone may instruct you to read the Word and stress how it is your lifeline. So, you begin. You start the routine of going to Sunday services. You sit in church, watching people stirred by the Spirit, yet you do not fully understand what is happening.

The same is true when you open your Bible. The words are there, but they feel distant. Some verses speak of grace, others seem to demand works. It does not take long before you start feeling like you cannot keep up.

You hear different ones say, *"God is pleased when you live holy,"* but then you read that *"you are made righteous by faith, not works."* One moment you hear, *"If you love God, you will keep His commandments,"* and the next you read that *"Christ is the end of the law for righteousness to everyone that believeth."*

Which is it? Do you have to earn it, or is it a gift?

This is where many new believers get stuck. They want to follow God, but they are not sure how—so they just try to do it all. And without realizing it, they place themselves under a burden God never intended them to carry.

What Happens When You Do Not Learn to Rightly Divide the Word?

Without rightly dividing the Word, you may find yourself spiritually exhausted, trying to follow every command in the Bible without understanding which ones were for Israel under the law and which ones apply to you under grace. This often leads to guilt, where some days you feel close to God, but on others, you feel like a failure. You may constantly question your salvation, reading one verse that says grace is enough while another seems to say you must *"do better."* You begin to fear that one mistake could cause you to lose God's favor.

Paul knew this struggle well. He had spent years chasing righteousness through works—until grace changed it all.

This is why he warned:

Galatians 5:1 – *Stand fast therefore in the liberty wherewith Christ hath made us free, and be not entangled again with the yoke of bondage.*

Paul warned believers not to return to a system of works-based salvation, as the law only brought slavery to sin, while grace in Christ brings true freedom.

We know Paul was referring to the law as the *"yoke of bondage"* in **Galatians 5:1** because of the surrounding context. In **Galatians 4:21-31**, he contrasts the two covenants—Hagar representing slavery under the law and Sarah representing freedom through grace. Then, in **Galatians 5:2-4**, he explicitly warns that those who seek righteousness through circumcision (a symbol of the Mosaic Law) are obligated to keep the whole law and have *"fallen from grace."* This makes it clear that the *"yoke of bondage"* refers to trying to attain righteousness through the law instead of by faith in Christ.

If you do not learn to rightly divide the Word, you will constantly live entangled—trying to walk in grace while carrying the weight of the law.

The Challenge: Letting Go of a Law-Based Mindset

Many believers struggle to fully embrace grace because they have been conditioned to believe that righteousness comes through effort. Even after salvation, they feel they must work to maintain God's approval. Paul confronted this directly:

Galatians 5:4 – *Christ is become of no effect unto you, whosoever of you are justified by the law; ye are fallen from grace.*

While Christians today do not follow the Mosaic Law, many live under modern-day laws—unspoken rules that make them feel they must **earn** what God has already freely given.

- **Moral Perfection** – Trying to be *"good enough"* rather than resting in Christ's righteousness.

- **Seeking Approval** – Measuring their faith by how others see them instead of how God sees them.

- **Spiritual To-Do Lists** – Feeling pressure to maintain routines to stay in God's favor.

- **Financial Pressure** – Linking God's favor to giving or success.

- **Past Mistakes** – Believing past sins still define them.

Paul made it clear that righteousness is by faith alone:

Titus 3:5 – *Not by works of righteousness which we have done, but according to his mercy he saved us.*

To break free from this mindset, believers must recognize when they are trying to earn what has already been given and stop measuring their worth by performance or approval. Instead of striving to be *"good enough,"* they must rest in Christ's finished work and renew their minds with the truth of grace, not man-made expectations.

Romans 6:14 – *For sin shall not have dominion over you: for ye are not under the law, but under grace.*

Living under grace means letting go of every form of legalism and embracing the freedom Christ has already provided.

3. Identity in Christ: Knowing Who You Are by Grace

Once a believer understands salvation and begins rightly dividing the Word, the next step in the Christian journey is discovering who they truly are in Christ. Many people accept Jesus but still live with an old mindset—seeing themselves as sinners, failures, or unworthy of God's love. But Paul teaches that when a person is saved, they receive a completely new identity.

2 Corinthians 5:17 – *Therefore if any man be in Christ, he is a new creature: old things are passed away; behold, all things are become new.*

Salvation is not just about going to heaven—it is about becoming a new person here and now. Grace does not just save; it transforms.

The Challenge: Letting Go of an Old Identity

Even after salvation, many people still see themselves through the lens of their past—mistakes, failures, or how they were raised. Their upbringing often shapes how they view themselves, especially if they were taught that righteousness was measured by following certain traditions or avoiding certain behaviors. Instead of identifying with their new nature in Christ, they continue to define themselves by their struggles, thinking, *"I'm just a sinner"* rather than declaring, *"I am the righteousness of God in Christ"* or saying, *"This is how we always did it,"* as if following a set way of living is what makes them right with God.

Their worth becomes tied to feelings instead of truth. But righteousness is not about feelings—it is a gift given by grace, not something to be earned or measured by past experiences.

Paul addressed this directly:

2 Corinthians 5:21 – *For he hath made him to be sin for us, who knew no sin; that we might be made the righteousness of God in him.*

Your righteousness is not based on behavior—it is a gift. If you keep identifying as a sinner, you will keep struggling with sin. But when you embrace your identity in Christ, your actions will follow.

4. Overcoming Trials: Grace Sustains You in Weakness

Even when a believer understands grace, challenges will still come. The Christian life is not free from hardship, but the difference is how we go through it. Grace is not just about salvation—it is the power that sustains us in difficult seasons.

Paul, who endured beatings, imprisonment, shipwrecks, and persecution, did not rely on his own strength. Instead, he leaned on God's grace:

2 Corinthians 12:9 – *And he said unto me, My grace is sufficient for thee: for my strength is made perfect in weakness.*

God never promised a trial-free life, but His grace is enough. Paul experienced this when he prayed for God to remove his *"thorn in the flesh,"* but instead, God assured him that His grace was sufficient.

This thorn was not a sickness, as some assume—Paul outlasted everyone but Jesus, continuing in ministry despite severe opposition. In context, the thorn in the flesh referred to people—false teachers, persecutors, and those who opposed the gospel. In **Numbers 33:55**, the phrase *"thorns in your sides"* was used to describe Israel's enemies, showing a biblical pattern of referring to hostile people as thorns. The phrase *"thorns in the side"* (or similar wording) appears in multiple places in the Bible, always referring to people—specifically enemies or adversaries who bring trouble and opposition. Paul was not battling an illness—he was facing relentless opposition, and God's answer was not to remove the hardship but to empower him to endure through grace.

The Challenge: Trusting Grace Instead of Your Own Strength

When faced with difficulty, the natural instinct is to try to fix everything alone, become frustrated and question God's plan, or feel defeated when things do not improve immediately. But Paul teaches that trials are not a sign of God's absence—they are opportunities to see His power at work, not in the sense that He is teaching you a lesson, as some understand it, but in the sense that His grace empowers you to endure and overcome.

Romans 5:3-4 – *We glory in tribulations also: knowing that tribulation worketh patience; And patience, experience; and experience, hope.*

Grace does not mean we will never struggle—it means struggles **will** **not** break us.

5. Walking in Victory: More Than a Conqueror by Grace

Paul did not just preach about *enduring* struggles—he preached about *overcoming* them.

Romans 8:37 – *Nay, in all these things we are more than conquerors through him that loved us.*

Being more than conquerors means we do not just survive difficulties—we overcome them through Christ. For years, I had repeated dreams of running and then suddenly taking off flying. These dreams were too frequent to count, stretching over nearly twenty years. But in every single one, the same truth remained: I knew I could fly. The feeling was so overwhelming, so vivid, that it stayed with me long after I woke up.

For years, I did not understand the meaning behind these dreams. It was not until I stepped into the knowledge of grace. One morning, after yet another of these dreams, I woke up as I had many times before. But this time, the Holy Spirit spoke: *"You have overcome."*

If you know me, you know my first reaction—I wanted to say, *"And You couldn't have just told me this years ago?"* It was a laughable moment, but in all seriousness, grace is what teaches you to walk in what He has already prepared for you so we each have a choice to step into grace, or not.

It was then I realized—those dreams had been showing me my struggle all along. I had spent years running, striving, and trying to take off on my own strength when, all along, I was meant to overcome and rise above it. But without understanding grace, I kept running in circles, wondering why I was still struggling. The moment I truly stepped into grace was the moment I realized I had already overcome.

The Challenge: Living Like a Victor Instead of a Victim

Some people, even after being saved, still live as if they are at the mercy of life's circumstances. They believe:

- *"The world is against me."*
- *"I will never get ahead."*
- *"My past still holds me back."*

But Paul reminds us that **nothing** can separate us from the victory we have in Christ:

Romans 8:38-39 – *For I am persuaded, that neither death, nor life, nor angels, nor principalities, nor powers, nor things present, nor things to come... shall be able to separate us from the love of God, which is in Christ Jesus our Lord.*

Victory is not about what happens to you—it is about what Christ has already done for you.

6. Extending Grace to Others: Living Out Grace in Relationships

Grace is not just something we receive—it is something we are called to extend. If grace transformed Paul, a former persecutor of Christians, into one of the greatest apostles, then it can transform the way we treat others.

Paul urged believers to let grace shape their words, attitudes, and relationships:

Colossians 4:6 – *Let your speech be **always** with grace, seasoned with salt, that ye may know how ye ought to answer every man.*

Paul uses salt to symbolize wisdom, discernment, and truth in speech. Just as salt enhances and preserves, our words should be filled with grace while carrying truth and wisdom that strengthen and uplift others. This uplifting is vital because, unlike the law, which condemns and burdens, grace edifies and brings life. Where the law pointed out failure, grace-filled speech points to redemption, hope, and the finished work of Christ. Grace does not just impact our relationship with God—it changes how we interact with people.

The Challenge: Overcoming Pride and Unforgiveness

One of the greatest struggles in relationships is forgiving and showing grace when people do not deserve it. When someone speaks harshly, the natural response is to lash out. If a friend betrays trust, the temptation is to cut them off completely. When a family member repeatedly hurts you, bitterness begins to take root. But Paul teaches that we forgive because we have been forgiven:

Colossians 3:13 – *Forbearing one another, and forgiving one another, if any man have a quarrel against any: even as Christ forgave you, so also do ye.*

Grace does not mean excusing sin or tolerating abuse, but it does mean releasing bitterness and trusting God to deal with situations.

7. Grace Until the End: Finishing the Race Well

Grace is not just for the beginning of the Christian Walk—it carries believers all the way to the finish. Paul did not just receive grace for salvation; he depended on it for his entire journey.

At the end of his life, Paul wrote:

2 Timothy 4:7 – *I have fought a good fight, I have finished my course, I have kept the faith.*

But Paul never could have finished the race if he had been running in his own strength. If his endurance had depended on works, doing good, or sheer determination, he would have failed.

The only reason Paul was able to complete his course was because he fully relied on grace.

1 Corinthians 15:10 – *But by the grace of God I am what I am: and his grace which was bestowed upon me was not in vain; but I laboured more abundantly than they all: yet not I, but the grace of God which was with me.*

Even Paul's labor—his preaching, his suffering, his missionary work—was not a result of human effort but the power of grace working through him.

Mama's Life—Carried by Grace

At Mama's funeral, many people reflected on who she was—loving, kind, outgoing, outspoken, heavily involved with youth, community, church, teaching, and serving in countless ways. From the outside, it may have looked like she was simply a person of great effort, constantly working to do good.

But those who truly knew her understood something deeper: none of it was done in her own strength.

Mama did not wake up every day *trying* to be strong, *trying* to be enough, or *trying* to make things happen by sheer effort. She often spoke of the vision God placed within her and leaned on His grace daily.

What many people did not see were the little moments—the times she sought God's direction, the quiet prayers, the trust she placed in Him when things were uncertain. Those unseen moments were what truly carried her.

She did not rely on herself. She relied on the grace of God, and that was what allowed her to finish her race well.

This is exactly what Paul was talking about when he said *"But by the grace of God I am what I am."*

Mama's life was a testimony to this truth: God's grace is enough—not just to start the race, but to finish it.

The Challenge: Not Giving Up When the Journey Gets Hard

Some believers start strong but grow weary because they try to finish in works what was started in grace, feel unworthy and doubt if they can make it, or believe it all depends on them. Paul reminded believers that the same grace that saved them would sustain them until the end:

Philippians 1:6 – *Being confident of this very thing, that he which hath begun a good work in you will perform it until the day of Jesus Christ.*

Paul finished his race not because he was strong, but because God's grace was sufficient. And that same grace is available to you.

The Sound of Silence: When Less Becomes More

Social Media, Grilled Cheese, Downton Abbey, Pepsi Products, and Coffee. What do these five things have in common? At first glance, not much. But as I wrote this book, I realized how much they shaped my journey to finishing it.

It started with a Christmas gift. My stepson, Twain, and his wife, Stephanie, bought us a tabletop grill, and I quickly put it to use. Before long, I was making grilled cheese sandwiches daily—so often they started tasting nothing short of restaurant style, if there is such a thing. My mama loved grilled cheese, and when she was living, she often asked me to make them for her. So, when Twain gave us that grill, it felt natural to fall into the routine. Before long, my husband was asking for one every day, and grilled cheese became a staple in our home.

At the same time, the Lord began pressing on me about distractions. Without realizing it, I had stepped away from social media months ago. I did not plan to fast from it; I just deactivated it. Looking back, I see how God led me to remove it without hesitation. Social media is not inherently bad, but in that season, I needed my heart and mind free from unnecessary noise so I could focus on what God was leading me to write.

But it was not just social media. As I neared the book's completion, I sensed I needed to be even more intentional. That is when I set aside my grilled cheese, Downton Abbey, and Pepsi products. Downton Abbey was the one show I genuinely enjoyed, but I knew it was time to let it go, at least for a while. The hardest thing to give up, though, was coffee. I have been a coffee lover for as long as I can remember, and it was one of my mama's favorites, too. In fact, when she regained the ability to speak after her stroke, one of the first things she said was, *"I want coffee."*

Laying these things aside may seem small, but that was exactly the point. I needed to position myself to hear God clearly, without anything—even trivial things—competing for my attention.

This all came to a head one night as I was making the final revisions. Chapter 16, *The Transformative Power of Grace*, felt off. It was not flowing, and I knew there was more the Lord wanted to say. Finally, I said, *"Lord, I am taking this out."* I deleted the entire chapter and began asking more questions about grace. But the Lord did not just give me answers—He gave me the questions that needed to be asked. The audible voice of God is unmatched!

By the time I went to bed the next morning, I had rewritten the entire chapter. The reason? I heard a word from Him.

It is easy to overlook the little things that pull at our time and attention, but sometimes, those are the very things standing in the way of what God is trying to do. Letting go of distractions—even small ones—creates space to hear Him more clearly. And when He speaks, everything shifts.

Hell? No!

Fear or Truth

What if I told you that sin does not send people to hell? Would you be shocked? Would you call it heresy? I can hear it—*"This is dangerous teaching! You are giving people a free pass to sin! You are leading them straight to hell!"* Before you react, take a breath, and stay with me. I challenge you—*do not just react, seek to understand.* Let us stick to scripture—not emotions, not traditions, not what we have always been told, but what the Bible actually says.

For over 30 years, I believed and was taught that sin sends people to hell. But then I studied the Word more deeply, and I saw something that shook me. The Bible does not say, *"If you sin, you will go to hell."* Instead, it says,

"He that believeth not is condemned already, because he hath not believed in the name of the only begotten Son of God." (**John 3:18**)

Stay with me. Sin separates people from fellowship with God, but what truly separates a person from God for eternity is not sin—it is **rejecting** the only One who can save. If sin alone sent people to hell, then why did Jesus die? Was His sacrifice not enough?

Ask yourself the question—or did He truly take away the sin of the world, as **John 1:29** says?

This is not about ignoring sin or excusing it—it is about **understanding grace properly**. If people truly grasp what Jesus did, they will not **want** to continue in sin. Grace is not a license to sin—it is the **power to overcome it**.

Grace Is NOT a License to Sin

Some people hear about grace and immediately panic. *"So, you are saying we can just do whatever we want? That sin does not matter?"*

Absolutely not!

That is not grace—that is deception. Grace does not lower the standard of holiness—it empowers us to live in it.

Paul makes it plain in **Romans 6:1-2**:

"What shall we say then? Shall we continue in sin, that grace may abound? <u>God forbid</u>. How shall we, that are dead to sin, live any longer therein?"

Grace does not excuse sin—it destroys its power.

This is unshakable: Jesus did not just die for sin—He died to end sin's dominion over us. If grace was a free pass to live however you want, then the cross was pointless. But the cross was not just about forgiveness—it was about *transformation.*

A Life That Truly Knows Grace Will Not Abuse It

When people ask, *"Can I keep sinning and still go to heaven?"* they are revealing their heart. The real question should be:

"How could I ever go back to what Jesus died to set me free from?"

Anyone who utterly understands grace does not ask, *"What can I get away with?"* They ask, *"How can I honor the One who gave everything for me?"*

That is where teaching the truth of Grace comes in. Because when you truly encounter grace, sin loses its appeal. <u>This is what Satan never wanted you to know</u>—that grace is not just about getting into heaven…it is about walking in heaven's power here on earth. This is not about legalism or rules. This is about living in the power of the resurrection. When you know who you are in Christ, you will not settle for sin—you will step into victory because **knowing** is the power that dominates it.

Eternal Separation

What does separate and condemn a person from God for eternity?

Rejecting Jesus.

God originally gave Adam and Eve **authority** over the earth (**Genesis 1:26**), but when they sinned, they lost that dominion. Jesus later referred to Satan as the ruler of this world (**John 12:31**). That is why Jesus came—not just to forgive sin, but to restore everything that was lost. **Luke 10:19** declares that through Him, our authority is restored.

Many misunderstand what the Bible teaches about sin and hell. I would ask you to find in the New Testament where hell is presented as punishment for sin itself. You will not—because hell is the consequence of rejecting Christ (**Revelation 20:15**). Under the New Covenant of grace, scripture makes it clear that our sins are forgiven (**John 3:17-18**), and we are reconciled to God through Jesus. Condemnation comes only from rejecting Christ, not from sin itself. Yet, for over two thousand years, more emphasis has been placed on sin than on grace—when the entire focus of the New Testaments is grace. When I saw this, I had to ask myself, *"How in the world did I miss this?"*

Sin: Before The Cross

Before Jesus, **sin created separation** between God and man.

Adam and Eve disobeyed God and were cast out of Eden. Israel's continued rebellion led to captivity, destruction, and loss. *Sin had consequences*, but the Old Testament **never** presents hell as the penalty—instead, people made sacrifices to maintain right standing with God.

The concept of Sheol (the grave) appears in the Old Testament, but it is not described as eternal torment. Instead, sin was something that had to be atoned for, pointing forward to Jesus as the ultimate sacrifice.

Old Testament Judgment

Several passages reference **Sheol or '*hell,*'** but they do **not** describe eternal punishment for sin:
- **Isaiah 14:9-11** – *"Hell from beneath is moved for thee to meet thee at thy coming..."*
(Context: This refers to the fall of the king of Babylon, describing Sheol as a place of the dead—not eternal punishment.)
- **Psalm 9:17** – *"The wicked shall be turned into hell, and all the nations that forget God."*
(Context: This speaks of judgment for rejecting God, not eternal torment for sin.)
- **Proverbs 15:24** – *"The way of life is above to the wise, that he may depart from hell beneath."*
(Context: This emphasizes that following God leads to life, not eternal damnation.)

The Old Testament's focus was never about eternal punishment for sin. It was about separation—how sin distanced people from God, requiring ongoing sacrifices for atonement.

The New Testament's Shift

When Jesus came, He **clarified** what hell really is—**a place of eternal separation from God**, not a punishment for sins that have been atoned for.

John 3:18 says:
"He that believeth not is condemned already, because he hath not believed in the name of the only begotten Son of God."

Jesus took care of **sin completely** (**Hebrews 10:4**), and now the issue is no longer *what we have done* but **whether you accept or reject Him.**

Hell Revealed

- **Revelation 20:15** – *"And whosoever was not found written in the book of life was cast into the lake of fire."*

(Hell is the destination of those who reject Christ—not a direct punishment for sin itself.)

- **Revelation 21:8** – *"But the fearful, and unbelieving, and the abominable… shall have their part in the lake which burneth with fire and brimstone: which is the second death."*

(These people are separated from God because they did not receive Christ, not because of individual sins.)

- **Matthew 25:41** – *"Depart from me, ye cursed, into everlasting fire, prepared for the devil and his angels."*

(Hell was originally created for Satan and his demons, but those who reject Christ share in that separation.)

You Are Not Your Flesh

It is often said, *"No sin will enter in,"* and while that is true, it is important to understand what that really means. That statement is not referring to your **body**—it's referring to your **spirit**.

Think about it: if a believer backslides and the Lord returns at that exact moment, will they go to hell? Many would instinctively say *yes*. But if that were the case, then another question must be asked—*what about you?*

Imagine a man who once walked closely with God but, over time, stopped going to church. Someone later hears that he has started gambling again, and suddenly, the whispers begin—*"He's backslidden."* If Jesus returned in that moment, would he be condemned? Some would say yes.

What if, at the very moment Jesus returns, you are unknowingly committing a sin? Would you be condemned as well? Most would say no. But why? Scripture is clear—there is no distinction between sin (**James 2:10**), and it also tells us that we all sin unknowingly (**Psalm 19:12**).

Yet, many hold to the belief that some sins will send a person to hell while others will not and moreso if they are in a backslidden state—not because scripture says so, but because it is what they were taught.

If all sins are equal (**James 2:10**), then why do people classify some sins as more damning than others? The truth is this belief is not rooted in grace or scripture—it is rooted in tradition. Many have been taught that certain sins mark a person as *"backslidden,"* while everyday struggles are dismissed as human weakness such as overeating, gossip, lying and manipulation of others.

But scripture makes no such distinction. If salvation were based on whether a person had any unconfessed sin at the moment of Christ's return, then no one could be saved—because no one walks perfectly in the flesh.

Your Flesh and Your Spirit Are Not the Same

This means even the best human effort **falls short** of God's standard. No amount of personal holiness, striving, or religious discipline can qualify a person for heaven. But here is the good news:

- Your identity is not in your flesh—it is in your spirit.

- Your spirit has been made righteous through Christ.
  Paul explains this struggle in **Romans 7:17-20**:
  "Now then it is no more I that do it, but sin that <u>dwelleth</u> in me... For the good that I would I do not: but the evil which I would not, that I do."

Paul is not excusing sin; he is **making a distinction—sin still operates in the flesh, but the born-again spirit is already righteous in Christ (2 Corinthians 5:21).**

Your Spirit Is Righteous—Your Flesh Is Not

The reason your **flesh will not enter heaven** is because it remains corrupted by sin.
1 Corinthians 15:50 confirms this:
"Now this I say, brethren, that flesh and blood cannot inherit the kingdom of God; neither doth corruption inherit incorruption."

Your flesh—your human body—**is not redeemed yet**. That is why Paul speaks about the **transformation** that will take place at the resurrection:
"We shall not all sleep, but we shall all be changed, in a moment, in the twinkling of an eye, at the last trump..." (**1 Corinthians 15:51-52**).

At that moment, believers will receive a new, glorified body, free from sin and corruption.

God's Home Is Not Condemned.

I used to work as an inspector, evaluating homes. Some were in such bad shape that I would not let my dog live in them.
If a home is condemned, it is unfit for occupancy.
That made me think—why would God choose to live inside us if we were still condemned?

But what you need to know is this: He does live in us—because you **are** no longer condemned.

"Know ye not that ye are the temple of God, and that the Spirit of God dwelleth in you?" (**1 Corinthians 3:16**).

If God Himself dwells in us, then condemnation is impossible—because He would never live in something unclean. God resides in you and that is why the Bible says Satan trembles!

Why Hell Fears YOU!

Let us stop tiptoeing around this truth. Sin exists in the flesh, but you are not your flesh. You no longer have to act as if you belong to it or walk as though sin has power over you. Shame and guilt have no right to suffocate your boldness. You are not some weak, barely-holding-on believer. You are not chained to your past and you are not fighting for righteousness—you already have it.

Hell has no claim on you. Condemnation has no claim on you. Satan has no claim on you.

The enemy's greatest fear is that you will wake up to who you truly are in Christ—righteous, redeemed, and victorious. He thrives on deception, hoping you will still believe you are bound when Christ has already set you free. I do not want to keep saying the moment you stop seeing yourself as a slave to sin and start walking in the power of grace, hell loses its grip, but it is true, and you just have a choice to make at this point.

Hell just does not fear a believer who is unsure or constantly questioning their standing with God. Hell fears a believer who knows they are already victorious and that is exactly who you are and THAT RIGHT THERE is why hell fears YOU.

Jesus did not just die to get you to heaven one day—He brought heaven into you now.

Hell is not trembling at people who just go to church. Hell does not tremble at people who try to be good. Hell trembles at believers who **know their authority**!

This is why Satan fights so hard to keep believers trapped in guilt and unworthiness. This is why he lies and whispers, *"You're not good enough. You are still struggling. God must be disappointed in you."*

The enemy knows how dangerous you are. That literally could have been the title of the book and the whole narrative all in one. Satan knows you are dangerous because the believer who walks in grace, without condemnation, without fear?

That is the one the devil cannot stop.

Neither Do I Condemn Thee

Jesus did not just free us from sin—He freed us from condemnation. Still, far too many believers remain bound in shame—not because God has not forgiven them, but because people will not let them forget. The weight of past mistakes lingers not because grace is not available, but because judgment has been given a longer shelf life than Jesus ever allowed.

Divorce is one of the most misunderstood and weaponized topics in church. Some view it as an unforgivable failure, a stain that permanently disqualifies a person from leadership. But does God see it that way?

When the religious leaders dragged a woman caught in adultery before Jesus, they expected condemnation. Instead, they were met with grace:

"Neither do I condemn thee: go, and sin no more." **(John 8:11)**

If Jesus Himself did not condemn her, why are some so quick to condemn others today?

If God calls a person to preach, to lead, or to serve in a higher capacity, does their past mistake override God's calling?

Does the blood of Jesus cleanse everything—except divorce?

Does Divorce Disqualify You from Leadership?

Many have been told that divorce permanently disqualifies them from serving in ministry, often based on a misinterpretation of **1 Timothy 3:2**: *"A bishop then must be blameless, the husband of one wife…"*

The Greek phrase *mia gune andra* (translated *'husband of one wife'*) does not mean a leader can never have been divorced. It simply means a man should be **faithful to his wife**—devoted to her, not given to adultery or polygamy. The early church was dealing with rampant immorality, and Paul was addressing faithfulness, not disqualification due to past mistakes.

Polygamy was common in the Old Testament, even among men God used mightily. Abraham, Jacob, David, and Solomon all had multiple wives, yet they were chosen for significant roles in God's plan. Abraham fathered nations yet took Hagar alongside Sarah (**Genesis 16**). Jacob, the father of the twelve tribes of Israel, had two wives and two concubines (**Genesis 29-30**). David, a man after God's own heart, had multiple wives (**2 Samuel 5:13**), and Solomon exceeded them all with *seven hundred wives and three hundred concubines* (**1 Kings 11:3**).

Yet despite these men's failings in their marriages, God still used them. If polygamy did not disqualify them under the Old Covenant, how much more does grace restore under the New Covenant?

Consider David. He committed adultery, yet God still used him. Peter denied Jesus three times, yet he became the foundation of the early church. Paul persecuted believers before becoming one of the greatest apostles. Nowhere does Scripture say that past failure, including divorce, overrides God's calling on a person's life.

The fact remains grace restores what religion disqualifies. If God still calls you, nothing can revoke that calling. Instead of looking at past failures, God looks at the heart. The question is not, *"Have you been divorced?"* but rather, *"Are you walking faithfully in Christ today?"*

What About Remarriage?

Many believers wrestle with whether remarriage is permissible, often due to legalistic interpretations of Scripture. Some point to **Luke 16:18**: *"Whosoever putteth away his wife, and marrieth another, committeth adultery..."* as proof that remarriage is always sinful. But is this what Jesus was really teaching?

Context Matters

Jesus was not establishing a new law—He was addressing the Pharisees' abuse of **Deuteronomy 24:1-4**, where men were divorcing their wives for trivial reasons. In that culture, a divorced woman had little to no financial or social security. These men were not divorcing due to broken marriages but for their own convenience, leaving their wives abandoned. Jesus was condemning heartless, selfish divorce—not forbidding remarriage altogether.

Paul's Teaching on Remarriage

Paul provides **clear guidance** in **1 Corinthians 7:27-28**: *"Art thou bound unto a wife? Seek not to be loosed. Art thou loosed from a wife? Seek not a wife. But and if thou marry, <u>thou hast not sinned</u>..."* This explicitly states that remarriage after divorce **is not a sin**.

Additionally, in **1 Corinthians 7:15**, Paul explains that if an unbelieving spouse leaves, the believer is **not bound** to the marriage, implying the freedom to remarry. Nowhere does Paul say that remarriage places a person in perpetual adultery.

God's Character: Redemption Over Condemnation

The heart of God is always **redemptive, not restrictive**. Jesus restored the broken, lifted the condemned, and freed people from bondage. If He extended grace to the woman caught in adultery (**John 8:11**), why would He reject someone simply for seeking love again after a failed marriage?

Legalism says, *"Once divorced, forever disqualified."* Grace says, *"Your past does not define your future."*

Final Thought:

Remarriage is not a sin—it is a restoration. Religion may cling to disqualification, but grace restores.

The question is not, *"Have you been divorced?"* The question is, *"Are you walking faithfully in Christ today?"*

David fell. Peter denied. Paul persecuted. Yet God still called them.

If your past mistakes could cancel God's calling, then grace would have no power. But grace does have power—power to redeem, the power to restore, and power to free you from the weight of the past.

So do not walk ashamed. Do not carry guilt for what God has already forgiven. If He has given you a new beginning, receive it fully—with faith, not fear.

Because God does not rewrite your story with regret—He rewrites it with redemption.

Staying Rooted in Grace

By now, you should be starting to understand your authority—not just in overcoming sin, but in walking free from condemnation. Grace has freed you from performance-based religion and placed you firmly in Christ. But here is the real question—how do you stay in that freedom?

The Subtle Drift Back to Performance

Paul warned believers about this very thing in **Galatians 3:3**:

"Are ye so foolish? Having begun in the Spirit, are ye now made perfect by the flesh?"

He was speaking to Christians who had already received grace but were drifting back into works-based righteousness. And is that not exactly what happens today?

One moment, you know you are fully accepted by God. But then, the enemy starts whispering:

- *"You should be praying more."*
- *"You haven't read your Bible enough."*
- *"Look at your struggles—are you sure you're really free?"*
- *"If you just tried harder, you'd be a better Christian."*

Before long, you are right back where you started—feeling like you have something to prove. Here is the hard truth: if Satan cannot keep you from grace, he will try to convince you that it is fragile—that you must maintain it through your own effort. But grace is not fragile. It is firm, unshakable, and eternal—because it was never based on you to begin with.

Recognizing the Signs

Legalism does not always look like strict rules. Sometimes, it disguises itself as *'discipline.'* It sounds like obedience but carries an undertone of fear and pressure. Here are some red flags that you might be slipping back into law-based thinking:

- Your joy in Christ starts to feel more like pressure to perform.
- You measure your relationship with God by how *'well'* you have been doing lately or how others perceive you.
- You feel like you have to *'make up'* for your mistakes before you can go to God.
- You find yourself comparing your spiritual walk to others.
- You feel distant from God, but instead of resting in grace, you try to *'fix it'* by doing more.

These subtle shifts are dangerous because they pull you away from the freedom you already have in Christ. They make you live as if grace is not enough—when it is.

Breaking Free from the Cycle

This cycle of striving does not always show up in obvious ways—it sneaks in through small moments. A slight guilt. A subtle pressure. A whisper that says you are not doing enough. Before you know it, you have slipped back into performance-based thinking, measuring your worth by what you do instead of who you are in Christ.

That is exactly what happened the other day. I pressed into writing instead of my usual study time—something God had clearly led me to do. Yet guilt crept in, whispering, *"You're off track."* I caught it instantly and laughed. Why? Because I had seen this pattern before.

And that is what breaking free looks like. It is not that you never stumble—it is that you catch yourself before condemnation takes root. The enemy does not have to make you fall into sin to make you ineffective. He just has to keep you stuck—worrying instead of trusting, striving instead of resting, overthinking instead of moving in faith.

The key is recognition. The moment you recognize the lie; its power is broken. Instead of dwelling on failure, celebrate the fact that you caught it—because that means grace is working in you.

Final Thought: Keep Standing in Grace

Grace is not fragile. It does not waver when you do. The moment you stop striving and rest in Christ's finished work, the cycle is broken. You do not have to fight for grace—it already holds you. Stand firm. You are free.

What If God Really Forgot?

What Does It Mean

"Remember Their Sins No More"

When God says in **Hebrews 10:17**, *"And their sins and iniquities will I remember no more,"* God knows everything—so it does not mean He *forgets* like we do when we misplace our keys. Instead, He chooses never to bring our sins up again.

This means that through Jesus, our record is wiped clean. You are not just forgiven—your sins are erased from the account entirely. But do you really believe that? Do you live as if God has truly removed your sins, or do you keep allowing Satan to drag them back up?

Seeing the Truth Beyond the Veil

Imagine standing in a gallery filled with paintings—each one depicting grace, freedom, and forgiveness. One shows chains breaking apart, symbolizing **Jeremiah 31:34**—*"I will forgive their iniquity and remember their sins no more."* Another shows a man standing in light, reflecting **Romans 8:1**—*"There is now no condemnation for those in Christ Jesus."* But something feels off. A thin veil separates you from the paintings. You can see them, you

can describe them, but they do not feel real.

That is what happens when you hear about God's grace but do not fully accept it. The words are right in front of you, but you do not step into the truth.

God does not bring up our past. He does not keep a list of our failures. God is not waiting to remind us of everything we have done wrong.

Imagine standing in a courtroom, knowing you are guilty. But instead of handing down a sentence, the judge wipes the record clean. No probation, no conditions—just completely cleared. That is exactly what Jesus did.

There is no need to walk around like we are still on trial.

"As Far as the East Is from the West"

God does not just cover our sins—He removes them. *"As far as the east is from the west, so far hath he removed our transgressions from us."* (**Psalm 103:12**)

If you travel north, eventually you will hit the North Pole and start heading south. But if you travel east, you will never reach west—they never meet. That is how far God has removed our sins from us.

That is grace. That is the power of Jesus' sacrifice. That means the moment you received Christ; your sins were permanently erased. Now that you know they are gone, there is no need to still live like they are following you.

Paid In Full

Believers do not have to live as if they are still under judgment—**Romans 8:1** says *there is now NO condemnation for those in Christ Jesus.*

And yet, that is how some Christians treat sin. They have been set free, yet they live burdened—apologizing for what has already been paid for and striving to fix what has already been erased.

The Challenge: Will You Accept Your Sins Are Gone?

Hebrews 10:17 is true. You no longer have to live like your past is hanging over your head.

Do you believe that Jesus truly erased your sins, or do you keep trying to *'make up'* for them? Do you live free, or are you still dragging around chains that have already been broken? This cannot be ignored: If you are in Christ, your sin does not exist in God's eyes. He has removed it, erased it, and will never bring it up again.

So, who is reminding you of it?

It is **not** *God.*

Final Thought: What If God Really Did Forget?

If He has erased your sins, why live like they still exist?
If He has removed your sins as far as the east is from the west, then you can *rest* in knowing they are gone.
If He has declared you not guilty, then there is no longer need to defend yourself.
The work is finished. The record is wiped clean. The debt is paid in full.

So, live like it.

Anointed, Not Appointed

The Anointing is for You—Not Just a Select Few.

If you have ever said, *'The anointing makes the difference,'* you are absolutely right. The anointing has often been viewed as something reserved for an elite group—pastors, evangelists, or those seen as *'spiritually special.'* But the truth is, every believer in Christ who has received the Holy Ghost is anointed.

A Shift from the Old to the New

Under the Old Covenant, the anointing was external and temporary, given only to specific individuals—kings, priests, and prophets—for specific tasks.
- David was anointed as king (**1 Samuel 16:13**).
- Aaron was anointed as high priest (**Exodus 29:7**).
- Elisha received the mantle of Elijah (**2 Kings 2:9-14**).

What is the Anointing?

The anointing is the Holy Spirit Himself, empowering you to fulfill God's will. It is not a separate *'thing'* from God, and it is not something you *'catch'* like a cold. The anointing is the power of the Holy Ghost moving in you—not just in moments of worship, but in daily life, decision-making, and authority over darkness.

Isaiah 10:27 gives a crucial truth about the anointing: *"And it shall come to pass in that day, that his burden shall be taken away from off* *thy shoulder, and his yoke from off thy neck, and the yoke shall be <u>destroyed</u> because of the anointing."*

This scripture shows that the anointing is a yoke-destroying power. Some, however, associate the anointing with a moment rather than a position. The anointing is not an event—it is a state of being. It is the empowered life of a believer.

What the Anointing Does in Your Life

The Holy Ghost anointing is not passive—it is active, powerful, and supernatural. When you recognize and walk in it, here is what happens:

1. The Anointing Gives You Power Over the Enemy

Jesus made this clear in **Luke 10:19**: *"Behold, I give unto you power to tread on serpents and scorpions, and over all the power of the enemy: and nothing shall by any means hurt you."*

- The anointing is not just for defense—it is for offense.
- The anointing does not just help you survive attacks—it makes you untouchable.
- The anointing is not for running from the enemy—it is for crushing him under your feet.

Demons feared Jesus because He walked **fully** in His anointing. And this is why Satan works overtime to keep believers ignorant of their own power. He knows that the second you understand the authority you have, you become unstoppable.

2. The Anointing Breaks Bondage in You—and Through You

"The Spirit of the Lord is upon me, because he hath anointed me to preach the gospel to the poor; he hath sent me to heal the brokenhearted, to

preach deliverance to the captives, and recovering of sight to the blind, to set at liberty them that are bruised." (**Luke 4:18**)

Jesus walked in the anointing not just for Himself, but for others. That same anointing is in you—even if you do not always feel it.

- When you step into a room, you bring the presence of God with you—whether you feel it or not. It is not falling from above or even filling a room in some external way. It is in you.
- When you pray, heaven listens—not because of how strong you are, but because of Who lives in you.
- When you speak, the enemy takes notice—not because of your confidence, but because of the authority Jesus has given you.

Satan fears anointed believers—not because they are perfect, but because they trust the One who lives in them. A believer who knows they are anointed is a threat to darkness. Hell, fears anointed believers who know who they are.

3. The Anointing Teaches and Guides You

"But the anointing which ye have received of him abideth in you, and ye need not that any man teach you: but as the same anointing teacheth you of all things..." (**1 John 2:27**)

The anointing is not just power—it is divine wisdom and guidance.

The Holy Spirit teaches, leads, and corrects you so that you can walk in victory. This is why anywhere you hear teaching or preaching and the anointing is not present, it will not transform you.

- Anointing brings revelation.
- Anointing brings clarity.
- Anointing makes the Word come alive.

That is why you do not just read the Bible—you read it under the anointing, allowing the Holy Spirit to teach you. This does not mean we do not need teachers or preachers. **Ephesians 4:11-12** makes it clear that God has given apostles, prophets, evangelists, pastors, and teachers to equip and build up the body of Christ. Their role is to help believers grow in their understanding and walk in their calling, but ultimately, the Holy Spirit is our greatest teacher.

Walking in Your Anointing

You do not need more power—you need to recognize what you already have. Stop waiting for a *'greater anointing'*—walk in what is already yours. The more you act in faith, the more you see its power.

Final Thought: You Are Anointed

You do not need a title or pulpit to be anointed. The anointing is not something you receive from others—it is the power of the Holy Spirit within you. The only thing stopping you from walking in your anointing—is you. So, step into it and as you do you will: Walk boldly. Speak with authority. Heal the sick. Cast out demons. Proclaim the Gospel. Set captives free.

The same Spirit that raised Jesus from the dead lives in you (**Romans 8:11**).

And that, right there? It makes hell tremble!

The Law Is Not Destroyed

When Jesus said, *"Think not that I am come to destroy the law, or the prophets: I am not come to destroy, but to fulfill"* (**Matthew 5:17**), He made it clear—the law was not eliminated, but its purpose had changed. He fulfilled every requirement of the law perfectly, meaning believers are no longer judged by it. But if the law is not destroyed, does that mean it still plays a role in the life of a believer today? And if so, what is its proper use?

Believers sometimes struggle with this balance. Some completely discard the law, believing it is irrelevant. Others hold onto it so tightly that they unknowingly live under legalism. The key is understanding the law's purpose, how Jesus fulfilled it, and what that means for us today. The law was never given to make people righteous. It was given to **expose** sin and prove that, apart from God, humanity could never reach His holy standard. **Romans 3:20** says, *"For by the law is the knowledge of sin."* The law exposed human brokenness, proving that righteousness could never be earned. It acted like a mirror, reflecting sin but offering no solution to remove it.

Stopping Legalism Before It Creeps In

Legalism is sneaky. It does not always show up as rules carved into stone or Old Testament commands being preached from the pulpit. It shows up in the small shifts of thinking that replace grace with performance.

It sounds like:

- *"If you really loved God, you would prove it by…"*

171

- *"You are saved by grace, but staying in God's favor depends on…"*
- *"God will bless you if you do your part."*
- *"You are only forgiven if you truly repent every time you sin."*

It creates an unspoken pressure to measure up—to do more, be more, prove more—as if Jesus' finished work needs our help.

And once that mindset takes hold, it leads to guilt, exhaustion, and a constant fear of not being enough. I know this firsthand. For years, I lived caught between law and grace, exhausting myself trying to please God. I believed in grace, yet deep down, I felt like I had to prove myself worthy of it. I read my Bible daily, attended services, worked in youth ministry, gave to those in need—doing everything I thought would keep me right with God.

But no matter how much I did, it never felt like enough. And then I hit my breaking point. Imagine if the Pharisees had been there. They would have stood over me with their list of rules, pointing out exactly why I was failing. I had not prayed enough, fasted enough, tithed enough, or strived hard enough. They would have reminded me of everything I had left undone, every way I had fallen short. And worst of all, they would have made me believe that God was just as disappointed in me as they were..

But that was not what happened. Instead of being met with judgment, I was met with grace. I had nothing left to give. I came home in tears, called my aunt, and admitted, *"I can't do this anymore."* Yet, in that moment, God was not disappointed. He did not scold me for not trying harder. He did not demand more effort.

He showed me grace—not as a doctrine, but as an experience.

Grace is not a transaction. It is not something you work to maintain. It is the unshakable reality of Christ's finished work. And that is exactly why legalism is so dangerous—because it makes you believe that grace is not enough.

How to Guard Against Legalism

Legalism is not always obvious. It starts subtly—just a little more effort, and a little more pressure—until it turns freedom into frustration. But the moment you recognize it creeping in, you can stop it.

- Remember that God's favor is not earned—only received. There is nothing you can do to make Him love you more or less.

- Reject thoughts that make righteousness about performance. Righteousness is not a reward—it is a gift (**2 Corinthians 5:21**).

- Stop striving and start trusting. You honor God not by proving yourself, but by **believing** Him.

- Check the fruit. If what you believe about God leads to exhaustion, fear, or guilt—it is not from Him (**Matthew 11:28-30**).

- Ask yourself: Am I doing this from love or from pressure? Grace always leads to joy, peace, and freedom—never burden.

And if you catch yourself falling into the *"try harder, do more"* trap, stop right there. God does not want more effort—He wants your trust.

The Law Fulfilled

Jesus gave the answer many searches for when asked about the greatest commandment. He did not point back to the 613 laws of the Old Testament. Instead, He summed it up in two simple commands:

"Thou shalt love the Lord thy God with all thy heart, and with all thy soul, and with all thy mind... and thou shalt love thy neighbor as thyself." (**Matthew 22:37-39**)

Love fulfills the law—not by replacing righteousness, but by producing it from the inside out. When you love God, you desire to walk in His ways. When you love people, you naturally treat them with grace, honesty, and kindness. Everything the law tried to produce through rules and regulations, grace accomplishes through relationship.

That is why Paul made it clear:

"But if ye be led of the Spirit, ye are not under the law." (**Galatians 5:18**)

This does not mean you live lawlessly—it means you live in the freedom of the Spirit, which produces holiness in a way the law never could.

Final Thought: Faith, Not Law, Pleases God

The Pharisees tried to enforce the law perfectly but missed the point—faith.

Jesus rebuked them, saying:

"Woe unto you, scribes and Pharisees, hypocrites! For ye pay tithe of mint and anise and cummin, and have omitted the weightier matters of the law, judgment, mercy, and faith..." (**Matthew 23:23**)

They obsessed over minor rules while neglecting what truly mattered—mercy and faith.

Righteousness is not earned through rule-keeping; it is received through faith in Christ. The Spirit within you produces what the law never could. You do not honor God by striving—you honor Him by believing.

The law is not destroyed—it is fulfilled in Jesus. And that is the difference between striving and freedom.

The Other Side of Submission

As I woke up this morning, God gave me a vision—not like my normal dreams. I was fully awake.

I saw myself walking beside a fence. It was not high, just a little over my waist. I could have easily climbed over it, but I did not. Instead, I kept walking in a straight line, always looking over to my right, seeing what was on the other side, but never crossing over. The strange thing was nothing was stopping me. There was no lock, no wall, no barrier holding me back—except me.

I could see everything on the other side, and I longed to go over, but I just kept walking beside it, as if I had accepted that this was the path I had to take. And it was not long before the Holy Spirit revealed—this was how I had spent most of my life. Always knowing there was more. Always seeing what was possible. But never stepping into it. The fence was not put there to keep me out. I just never opened the gate.

Looking back, I see how much of my life was lived in lack—not just emotionally, but spiritually, financially, and even physically. We faced the same struggles as others' health concerns, financial setbacks, and immaturity in relationships and for so long, I did not understand why. I was doing what I thought was right, yet something was missing. The problem was not that God was distant, but that I had never truly learned how to die to my flesh and submit fully to Him. This is exactly what **James 4:7-8** speaks of:

Submit yourselves therefore to God. Resist the devil, and he will flee from you. Draw nigh to God, and he will draw nigh to you. Cleanse your hands, ye sinners; and purify your hearts, ye double minded.

I thought I was submitting to God because I was doing *'good'* things—paying tithes, trying to be a good person, and avoiding sin. But submission is not just about action; it is about surrender. It is about laying down your own understanding, your fears, your wants, and fully trusting Him.

Total Submission

What is absolute total submission? Is that a question you have ever asked yourself? Well, I did not ask it—but I found out the hard way. I was in one of the hardest trials I had ever faced. And we have all been hurt before, so that part is not unique.

But this time, I was on my knees, crying out to the Lord. I said, *"God, you've got to do something."*

And as though He was standing right there, I heard Him say, *"I already have."*

Well, I kept crying and pleading—because apparently, He was not hearing me right. I mean, I was still hurting! So, I cried even more in desperation.

After what seemed like an eternity, I broke down and asked, *"Jesus, what do You want me to do?"*

And, clear as day, He said, *"Submit."*

I said, *"What do You mean submit? I am submitting."*

And He said, *"No, you are not."*

The Turning Point: When Submission Became Real

If people are going to learn valuable lessons, sometimes that means being transparent.

I could easily write about all the happy times, make it seem like I have always lived this grand, wonderful life, and tell you that you can too—just follow everything we have discussed.

Or… I can be real.

Because this is life about which we are talking. And in life, you are going to go through some crazy, crazy stuff. I have faced some attacks over the years that felt like nothing short of trying to take me out. But the key difference is learning to step over them with authority.

That is the price behind closed doors—the battles no one else sees, the moments when standing feels impossible, and the choice to keep going when everything in you wants to quit.

This was several years ago, and I was struggling hard. Satan was trying to wreak havoc in our marriage. Mark saw things one way, and I saw things another. And it became so hurtful that I did not know what to do. I loved him. He loved me. But at the time, our disagreement seemed bigger than anything we had ever faced. So, there I was, on my knees, begging and crying to the Lord.

And then, I heard Him say the word again: *"Submit."*

And I said, with a big, crying voice, *"I am submitting! Lord, do You want me to just continue to hurt? What about what I am going through? Lord, do You want me to submit to that?"*

And He said, *"No."*

And for those of you who remember the sitcom *Different Strokes*, I looked up, mid-cry, and said, *"What are you talking' 'bout, Lord?"*

Because I knew His Word. He said, *'Wives, submit unto your husbands.'* And God does not contradict His Word.

So, I let out another bellowing cry and said, *"Lord, what do You mean?"*

And He said, *"I need you to submit… to Me."*

Well, I cried even more because I thought I already had been. This went on for a little while longer and eventually I knew I had to make a choice to either trust Him or stay where I was with constant bouts of crying. That was a defining turning point—not only in my marriage but in my life.

It was in that moment that He told me, *"It is not about you."*

I did not understand it all then, but as time passed, I learned what **James 4:7-8** truly meant.

I had to die to my flesh.

I had to die to offenses.

I had to die to all that mess that keeps a person bound to feelings and emotions. Because let me tell you something—that junk will kill you. Or at the very least, it will steal your joy.

These things I have written about all come from experience. Just this week, while studying *Acts*, I read something in the commentary that hit me:

"We must not make the tragic spiritual mistake of 'teaching the experiences of the apostles,' but rather 'experience the teachings of the apostles.'"

That stuck with me. Because what better teacher is there than experiencing the truth for yourself? When you walk through trials and God reveals Himself in the middle of them, that is when you truly learn who He is.

I can honestly say that Jesus taught me something through that season—no matter what trial I face in this life, it is never about me. And let me tell you, that was one of the hardest, bittersweet pills I have ever had to swallow.

But now?

Now, I can say with boldness and confidence that we are truly living our best life in Him! Every day feels like a honeymoon. That does not mean trials do not come, but the difference is undeniable—what once took weeks to overcome is now settled in mere moments. We have learned to walk in dominion. Because here is the truth: whether in marriage, relationships, or life in general, it does not matter if you are the offender or the offended. Somebody reading this—maybe a young couple, maybe an older couple, maybe just someone who has not learned yet, needs to hear this.

Letting Go

Letting go of my own way meant surrendering how I thought things should be. It meant choosing to love even when it felt impossible, forgiving when I did not want to, and trusting that God's plan was greater than my emotions. Submission is not about weakness—it is about power under control. It is about dying to self so that Christ can truly live through you. When I finally humbled myself before Him, the battle with people faded, and my focus shifted fully to God. That is when I understood—

It is not about me at all.

24

Clean Heart, Not Just a Clean Cup

Dying to self does not just change how you respond to people—it changes how you see everything, including worship. Once I let go of my own way, I started noticing how much faith had been shaped by tradition instead of transformation.

Discussions about faith often bring out strong opinions, especially from those who are deeply committed to their beliefs. While their intentions may be sincere, their comments about how worship should look or how faith should be expressed can sometimes feel more like expectations than encouragement. These perspectives, though well-meaning, can unintentionally shift the focus from a genuine relationship with God to outward appearances, traditions, or personal preferences.

But true worship is not about meeting a checklist: it is about the heart. God is not looking for performance; He is looking for connection. When you focus on Him rather than the expectations of others, you find the freedom to worship in spirit and truth, unhindered by the weight of tradition or the fear of judgment.

The Heart Over Tradition

Early in my Christian Walk, I noticed how these expectations from others would bother my mama—not because she doubted their sincerity, but because she believed that every believer worshipped Jesus in their own way, even if their outward expressions differed. She would often remind my sister and me, *"The Christian walk is a growing process."* I did not fully grasp what she meant at the time, but I realize now that she was speaking from wisdom beyond her years.

There is a danger in placing too much emphasis on outward displays of faith. When religious traditions and external expressions become the standard for measuring spirituality, the true essence of a personal relationship with Christ can be lost. Jesus Himself confronted this issue with the Pharisees, who were more focused on their religious image than on their inner transformation.

In **Matthew 23:25-28**, Jesus rebuked them:

"Woe unto you, scribes and Pharisees, hypocrites! for ye make clean the outside of the cup and of the platter, but within they are full of extortion and excess. Thou blind Pharisee, cleanse first that which is within the cup and platter, that the outside of them may be clean also."

Picture a beautifully polished cup, gleaming on the outside. At first glance, it looks flawless—until you peer inside and see grime and residue that have been left untouched. No matter how perfect it appears, what's inside is what really matters. This is how Jesus described the Pharisees—fixated on maintaining a religious image while neglecting the heart.

For years, I unknowingly did the same. I believed my dedication—my constant church attendance, my works for Christ, my service—was what made me right with God. I thought that as long as I was doing everything *'right'* on the outside, my relationship with God was in order. But just like that polished cup, I had not allowed God to fully cleanse the inside. A clean heart is not achieved through outward effort alone; it starts with an internal change that only He can bring.

Jesus was not calling for better appearances—He was calling for authenticity. True spiritual maturity is not defined by how you appear to others but by the genuine transformation of your heart and mind. Someone may teach, preach, or speak with confidence and eloquence yet lack authentic faith or spiritual depth. Conversely, a person who may not speak with confidence, conform to traditional expressions of worship, or possess polished eloquence can still be deeply rooted in faith and connected to God. Whether through quiet reflection or personal expressions, they may exemplify a Spirit-filled life. Outward appearances, after all, can be deceiving.

True Worship: More Than Outward Expression

Praise is more than a song, a shout, or a raised hand—it is an open invitation for God to move in your life. True worship is not just something you do; it is who you are. It is the posture of a heart that recognizes His presence, responds to His goodness, and remains connected to Him in every moment.

Psalm 34:1 says:
"I will bless the Lord at all times: his praise shall continually be in my mouth."

This verse is not about a temporary action—it is about a lifestyle of praise. Worship does not begin and end with a church service. It is carried in the way you think, the way you speak, and the way you live. As a believer, you have access to unceasing fellowship with God, where worship is not confined to moments of outward expression but becomes the very rhythm of your life.

Spiritual Maturity: An Internal Work

Spiritual maturity is a transformational process that begins in the heart. It is about growing in love, joy, peace, and the other fruits of the Spirit (**Galatians 5:22-23**), allowing them to shape our thoughts, actions, and responses. As you walk with God, your relationship with Him deepens, and your faith becomes less about what *you* do and more about who you are in Him.

For a long time growing up, I thought the scripture *"You will know them by their fruit"* referred to people who did all the right things—going to church every Sunday, volunteering, and serving in all capacities. But as I read it in context, I realized Jesus was not talking about outward actions; He was talking about the fruit within—love, long-suffering, kindness, and more.

At the core of this journey is love—the greatest of all (**1 Corinthians 13:13**). True maturity is reflected in how you love God and others, not out of obligation but from a heart that is fully aligned with His will. It is seen in the way you extend grace, seek understanding, and walk confidently in your identity in Christ, regardless of external pressures.

We all encounter people who challenge us—individuals we struggle to be around for various reasons. But have you ever stopped to ask why Jesus placed love at the very top of the fruits of the Spirit? It is because He knew that loving the seemingly unlovable would be one of the hardest things we would ever have to do. People can be relentless in their actions, thoughtless with their words, and difficult to love. And yet, Jesus calls us to love anyway—not because they deserve it, but because He first loved us (**1 John 4:19**). Walking in love is not always easy, but it is the clearest reflection of a heart that has been transformed by God.

Final Thoughts: Standing Firm in Grace

As believers, our worship and maturity are defined by our relationship with Christ. Whether in a congregation or in the quiet of our hearts, what matters most is that our worship is done in spirit and truth, reflecting God's grace and love.

God is not looking for performance. He is looking for hearts fully surrendered to Him. He is not impressed by outward expressions of worship if they do not reflect an inward transformation.

At the end of the day, the question is not whether you meet religious expectations—it is whether you are truly walking with Him.

Are you seeking to appear righteous, or are you allowing Him to transform you into righteousness?

Are you cleaning the outside of the cup, or are you letting Him cleanse you from the inside out?

God desires more than outward displays; He seeks hearts fully devoted to Him. And when the heart is truly transformed, the rest will follow.

Worship Beyond the Walls

Jesus said, *"But the hour cometh, and now is, when the true worshippers shall worship the Father in <u>spirit</u> and in <u>truth</u>: for the Father seeketh such to worship him. God is a Spirit: and they that worship him must worship him in spirit and in truth"* (**John 4:23-24**).

He spoke these words to the Samaritan woman at the well—an interaction that was significant. She was not a Jew; culturally, she was considered an outsider, someone the religious leaders of that time would have dismissed. Yet, it was to her that Jesus revealed one of the most foundational truths of the New Covenant: worship would no longer be about a place, but about the heart.

I did not fully grasp the weight of this truth until I looked at my own life. From my earliest memories, we were instructed not to enter the pulpit unless invited—much less to walk across it. There was an unspoken reverence attached to physical space, and I, too, followed suit, often telling others not to run across the stage. There is nothing wrong with teaching respect, but I realized I was more concerned with protecting the stage than reaching the people standing just outside of it. It was not until I came to know grace that I utterly understood holiness is not about a location; it is about who resides within you.

For so long, I had been conditioned to think certain places were holier than others and stepping onto a stage where sermons were preached required a special invitation, as if God's presence only rested there. But when I began to truly study the Word, I saw the shift Jesus introduced. Worship was no longer confined to a temple, a mountain, or a building. It was not about sacred ground—it was about **a sacred heart.**

The Jews and Pharisees placed great emphasis on where worship took place—the temple in Jerusalem being the only place they deemed acceptable. The Samaritans, on the other hand, worshipped on Mount Gerizim. This was the divide between them, and it was what the woman brought up in her conversation with Jesus. But He made it clear: a time was coming, and in fact, had already begun, when worship would not be tied to a physical location.

This was not just a passing statement; it was a shift in how people would relate to God. Under the Old Covenant, worship revolved around the temple, the sacrifices, and the priesthood. But Jesus was pointing to something greater—a direct relationship with God through the Spirit. Worship would not be about a building, a mountain, or a set of rituals. It would be about worshipping in spirit—a connection to God that is real, alive, and led by the Holy Spirit—and in truth, grounded in who God truly is, not in religious traditions or expectations.

Yet today, some believers still miss this; they hold onto the mindset that worship is about going to a certain place—a church building, a conference, or some special gathering—rather than understanding that true worship is about how we **approach** God. It is not about showing up at a location; it is about a life lived in surrender, guided by the Spirit, and aligned with truth. This was the foundation of the New Covenant, and Jesus revealed it to a Samaritan woman before most religious leaders ever grasped it.

Jesus was not contradicting Scripture or saying not to gather; believers are still called to come together. But it is **how** we gather that defines our relationship with Christ. Worship is not about checking a box or attending a service; it is about a heart truly engaged with God.

Understanding worship beyond a place also reshapes how we see assembling. It is not just about meeting together—it is about standing firm, growing, and strengthening one another in faith. This leads to an important discussion —what does it really mean to assemble as believers?

The verse **Hebrews 10:25**, *"Not forsaking the assembling of ourselves together, as the manner of some is; but exhorting one another: and so much the more, as ye see the day approaching,"* is often used to emphasize church attendance. But when you look deeper, you find that it wasn't about merely showing up for a service—it was about survival.

The early church faced intense persecution **because they accepted the New Covenant of grace** and rejected the old system of the law, and these believers were not just gathering for routine worship; they were holding onto each other for strength, encouragement, and endurance in faith. Some were tempted to return to Judaism for safety, to blend back into their old religious systems to avoid the suffering that came with following Christ. The writer of Hebrews was not scolding them for skipping a Sunday service—he was pleading with them not to abandon their faith in the face of fear.

When you understand the **urgency** behind this verse, it *shifts your perspective*. Assembling together was never about fulfilling an obligation—it was about standing firm in faith, strengthening one another, and remaining anchored in Christ, especially in challenging times.

The Power of Gathering

Jesus introduced a new way of worship, one that was not tied to rituals, locations, or traditions, and plenty struggled to accept it. The Pharisees rejected it outright, clinging to the law. The Jewish believers wrestled with letting go of their old way of worship. Even now, that struggle continues.

Many years ago, I thought being in church every time the doors were open meant I was right with God. But even in all my doing, something was missing. I was assembling, but I was not growing.

I remember when God started shifting my understanding. I had always loved learning, and in the late 1990s, I had a deep hunger to study healing. But it was not until around 2003 that I found a book by Kenneth E. Hagin about spiritual authority that ignited something in me. The more I sought God's Word, the more I started hearing Him speak, leading me down a path that looked nothing like what I expected. And the more I read while learning to discern, the more I realized that worship was not about attendance; it was about *relationship*.

It took me years to truly grasp what the scriptures were saying. It was not until I began to understand *grace* that everything began to click. Yes, gathering was important, but what mattered most was the condition of my heart, my understanding of His Word, and my ability to stand in faith beyond the church walls.

When I started drafting this book about two years ago, I began to wrestle with guilt near the end for not being as involved in church functions as before. But I knew that God had called me to focus on this. Some did not understand. However, obedience to God's call mattered more than meeting people's expectations, and this is where a lot of believers get stuck. **Hebrews 10:25** is often quoted as a command *to* gather, but few stop to ask *why* we gather.

*What is **Hebrews 10:25** Really About?*

The phrase *"as ye see the day approaching"* reminds us that our time here is limited. Jesus is returning, and the days are growing darker. The early believers did not gather just for tradition's sake; they gathered because they knew they needed each other to stand strong in faith.

When we come together, the scripture shows us that it is about:

- Encouraging one another to stand firm in faith.
- Uplifting each other in truth, not just habit.
- Equipping believers to walk in their authority.
- Preparing one another to disciple and share the gospel.

But let us be clear: assembling is not the end goal—it is the starting point.

Jesus did not gather His disciples just to teach them; He gathered them so He could send them *out*. Too often, people confuse attendance with growth. Simply showing up does not automatically produce transformation. Yet, some believers come to church expecting the pastor to do all the work—praying, teaching, studying the Word—while they remain passive listeners. But that was never God's design.

Scripture makes it clear that every believer is called to grow, study, and strengthen others.

"Study to shew thyself approved unto God, a workman that needeth not to be ashamed, rightly dividing the word of truth" (**2 Timothy 2:15**).

If we are not reading, applying, and growing in the Word ourselves, **how** can we be that encourager to others?

Hebrews 5:12 also reminds us, *"For when for the time ye ought to be teachers, ye have need that one teach you again which be the first principles of the oracles of God; and are become such as have need of milk, and not of strong meat."*

We are not meant to stay dependent on others for our spiritual growth. We are called to mature, to build one another up, and to contribute to the body of Christ—not just receive from it. **Hebrews 5:12** is a key scripture that exposes a problem in the body of Christ—believers who should have matured into teachers and leaders but are still stuck on the basics.

Breaking It Down

1. **"For when for the time ye ought to be teachers..."**

   - Spiritual growth was not just suggested—it was expected. These believers had been in the faith long enough that they *should* have been teaching others by now. But something was wrong—they were stagnant.

2. **"Ye have need that one teach you again..."**

   - Instead of progressing, they needed to be *re-taught* the basics. Think about a student who keeps repeating the same grade because they never fully grasp the material. These believers were still struggling with foundational truths rather than building upon them.

3. **"The first principles of the oracles of God..."**

- The *first principles* refer to elementary teachings—the fundamental doctrines of the faith. These are things like salvation, repentance, faith in God, and eternal judgment (which **Hebrews 6:1-2** lays out). These are not *bad* things, but they are the *starting point*, not the goal.

4. **"And are become such as have need of milk, and not of strong meat."**

- *Milk* represents the basic teachings—the things a new believer needs to survive spiritually.
-*Meat* (or solid food) represents deeper revelation—applying the Word, walking in spiritual authority, and **discerning truth** for yourself.
-The phrase *'have need of milk'* suggests that they had regressed. They *should* have been chewing on meat, but instead, they were still dependent on the basics.

Milk vs. Meat: Moving from Hearing to Applying

Many believers settle for spiritual infancy, staying on *milk* when they should be growing into *meat*. **Hebrews 5:12-14** says:

"For when for the time ye ought to be teachers, ye have need that one teach you again which be the first principles of the oracles of God; and are become such as have need of milk, and not of strong meat. For every one that useth milk is unskillful in the word of righteousness: for he is a babe. But strong meat belongeth to them that are of full age, even those who by reason of use have their senses exercised to discern both good and evil."

Milk vs. Meat: What is the Difference?

- Milk (Basic Teaching) → Foundational truths that sustain new believers (*salvation, repentance, faith, eternal judgment*).
- Meat (Mature Application) → Personal revelation and obedience that move you into spiritual authority (*walking in faith, discerning truth, applying the Word daily*).

A baby cannot live on milk forever. At some point, they must grow, chew, and eat solid food. Spiritually, the same is true—there is nothing wrong with *starting* with milk, but if years go by and you are still relying on someone else to feed you, something is off.

The Real Problem: Why So Many Stay on Milk

Many Christians remain spiritually dependent because they rely on pastors and teachers to do all the studying, praying, and seeking for them. They hear a sermon, nod in agreement, and say, *"That was a good word!"*—but then they never open their Bibles at home, never apply what they heard, and never grow past needing someone else to explain everything to them.

The issue? Milk alone will not sustain spiritual growth. **Hebrews 5:12** exposes this problem: countless believers should be *teachers* by now, yet they are still waiting to be *spoon-fed*.

The shift from milk to meat happens when believers take personal responsibility for their growth. Instead of just *listening*, they start reading, seeking revelation, and living out the Word.

The Challenge: Growing Beyond the Basics

These are not questions for anyone else to answer for you—they are questions for you to ask yourself.

- Am I relying solely on pastors and teachers, or am I taking time to study the Word for myself?
- Am I simply attending church, or am I actively applying what I have learned?
- Am I growing in my faith to the point where I can encourage, teach, and equip others, or am I still in a place of needing constant guidance?

Growth is a journey, and no one arrives overnight. But as you walk with God, His desire is for you to move deeper—to mature, to stand firm, and to become someone who strengthens others in their faith.

Final Thought: Grow, So You Can Feed Others

Jesus did not call us to just be students—He called us to become teachers and disciple others. The real test of spiritual maturity is not how much you know, but how much you apply. Do not settle for milk when you were meant to feast on the fullness of God's Word. It is time to grow.

Assembling With Purpose

Plain and simple, we need each other. Fellowship strengthens us. The early church gathered to be equipped and encouraged so they could go out and share the gospel of grace. Our gatherings should inspire and prepare us to carry Christ beyond the church walls or then we must ask ourselves: are we truly fulfilling His purpose?

Acts 2:46 says:
"And they, continuing daily with one accord in the temple, and breaking bread from house to house, did eat their meat with gladness and singleness of heart."

Notice that their fellowship was not limited to one place. They gathered in the temple *and* in their homes. Worship wasn't just something they did—it was how they lived.

Final Thought: Gather, Grow, and Go

Jesus assembled His disciples, taught them, and sent them out. He said, *"Go into all the world and preach the gospel."*

God has given you everything you need to grow and walk in His purpose. Each time you gather, it is an opportunity to be strengthened in faith, to be equipped for what He has called you to, and to deepen your walk with Him. Worship is not about routine—it is about transformation. Let what you receive take root, so you can live it out daily.

Worship is not about a location—it is about a *life surrendered to God*.

- We gather—not because it is expected, but to be strengthened in faith.
- We grow—not through attendance alone, but through applying the truth.
- We go—not just to share knowledge, but to live out the gospel daily.

When you assemble, it is not just about being present—it is about growing in truth so you can live it out daily. Because true worship does not stop when the service ends—it begins.

Out of the Shadows, Into His Rest

For generations, the Sabbath was observed as a day of physical rest—**a sacred pause from labor** meant to honor God. It was a command given to Israel, a day set apart to reflect on God as Creator and Redeemer. But in the New Testament, **Jesus introduced a radical shift**—one that moved the focus from a single day to a continual state of *spiritual rest* found in Him.

Imagine a man working tirelessly from sunrise to sunset, pushing himself beyond exhaustion. He believes that only by working harder will he prove his worth, secure his future, and find fulfillment. Finally, one day, someone places a chair beside him and says, *"Sit, rest—it's already taken care of."*

At first, he resists. How can he stop? After all, working nonstop seems like the only way to achieve success. But then, he realizes something—resting does not mean doing nothing; it means *trusting* that the work has already been completed on his behalf.

This is the *essence* of the Sabbath's transformation in Christ. In the Old Covenant, the Sabbath was about ceasing from physical labor. In the New Covenant, it is about ceasing from self-effort and resting in the finished work of Christ.

Hebrews 4:9-10 explains this shift:

"There remaineth therefore a rest to the people of God. For he that is entered into his rest, he also hath ceased from his own works, as God did from his."

The Sabbath was never meant to be about a day—it was a **shadow** of the greater rest that Jesus would provide. He fulfilled what the Sabbath pointed to, offering not just one day of rest but a life of resting in Him.

This shift is significant. Instead of a single day dedicated to physical rest, you are invited to live in a *state* of rest—trusting, relying, and abiding in Him every day. The Sabbath was never meant to be a pause from work; it was meant to point us to a Savior who would become our eternal rest.

The Old Testament Sabbath

In the Old Testament, the Sabbath was a command given to Israel, observed on the seventh day (Saturday), and set apart as holy. It was a day of rest, a reminder of God's work in creation and His deliverance of Israel from Egypt (**Exodus 20:8-11; Deuteronomy 5:12-15**). This day was to be kept sacred, a sign of the covenant between God and His people.

The Sabbath served its purpose in that time—it established a rhythm of dependence on God, reminding the Israelites that their provision came from Him. Yet, it was always meant to be **a foreshadowing of something greater**—the ultimate rest that would come through Jesus.

The New Testament Fulfillment in Christ

Jesus as Lord of the Sabbath

When Jesus walked the earth, He did something radical—He challenged the rigid traditions surrounding the Sabbath. The religious leaders had turned it into a burdensome rule, losing sight of its true meaning.

Matthew 12:8 records Jesus' declaration:

"For the Son of man is Lord even of the Sabbath day."

He was making it clear that the Sabbath was never about mere rule-following—it was about **Him**. He further clarified this in **Mark 2:27-28**:

"And he said unto them, The Sabbath was made for man, and not man for the Sabbath."

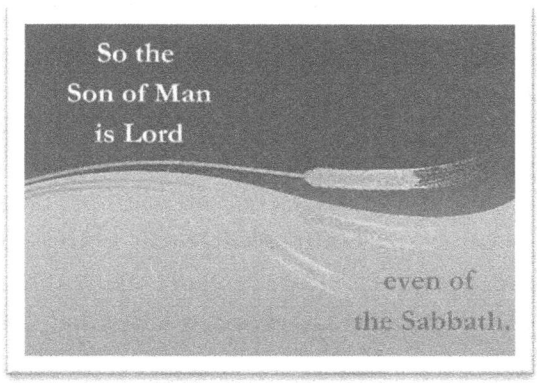

Jesus demonstrated this truth by healing on the Sabbath (**Luke 13:10-17**), revealing that the heart of the Sabbath was not restriction, but restoration. This was a pivotal shift—from a legalistic observance to a deeper understanding of rest found in Him.

Radical Shift for the Jews

For devout Jews, who had built their identity around observing the Sabbath, this change was difficult to accept. However, for those weighed down by heavy religious rules, it brought hope and freedom. Jesus revealed that He is the eternal Sabbath, offering complete peace with God.

Similarly, a lot of believers today equate Sunday with the *'new Sabbath,'* viewing it as a day of worship and rest. While there's value in setting aside time for God, the deeper truth lies in understanding that Jesus **Himself** is our Sabbath rest. It is about ceasing **self-effort under the law** in trying to attain righteousness, not about physically stopping work. Under the New Covenant, you **work from a place of rest, not for rest**. When you understand this, your efforts become an act of worship (**Colossians 3:23**)

Laboring to Enter Rest

Laboring to enter rest does not mean striving in the way the world defines labor. Instead, it is an intentional shift in trust—choosing to rest in what Christ has already done rather than relying on your own strength. **Hebrews 4:11** tells us to labor to enter that rest because it requires effort to resist the natural inclination to work for righteousness. The world teaches that attending service on Saturday or Sunday, or even working hard to prove one's devotion, is what brings rest, but God's rest is received through faith, not effort. Entering that rest means actively reminding yourself of His promises, surrendering anxious thoughts, and refusing to carry burdens that Christ has already borne. It is not about passivity but about continually anchoring yourself in the truth of God's grace, even when everything around you pushes you toward striving. True Sabbath rest is not found in a day but in Him.

Overcoming Unbelief

Laboring to enter rest is not just about ceasing from self-effort—it also means overcoming the unbelief that keeps us from fully receiving what God has already provided. Just as the Israelites failed to enter the Promised Land due to unbelief (**Hebrews 3:19**), we must guard against doubt and trust fully in God's promises.

Imagine someone drowning in debt, constantly stressed, and praying for financial breakthrough. They hear about God's provision but continue to operate in fear—working tirelessly, hoarding, and refusing to give because deep down, they do not genuinely believe God will take care of them. Their mindset keeps them in a cycle of striving instead of resting in the truth that *"My God shall supply all your need according to his riches in glory by Christ Jesus"* (**Philippians 4:19**). Just like the Israelites, their unbelief keeps them from stepping into the provision already made available.

Trusting God's promises requires action—choosing faith over fear, rest over striving, and obedience over hesitation. When you truly believe, you stop wandering in circles and start walking in His provision.

From Striving to Resting in Grace

Many Christians unknowingly approach their relationship with God by how much they do—reading the Bible, attending services, or praying enough to feel worthy. But true faith is not about checking off spiritual tasks; it is about abiding in Him. When you understand grace, these actions stop being obligations and become expressions of love. You pray because you desire connection, not because you fear disapproval. You read the Word because it nourishes you, not because it earns you favor. Instead of striving to be accepted, you rest in the reality that you already are.

I could ask the following:

- How many have a Bible in your home?
- How many pick it up and read it?
- How many read it daily?
- How many study and meditate on what you have read?
- How many have prayed and asked God to help you rightly divide the Word?

These questions may seem like simple prompts for self-reflection. But what message are they really relaying?

Although these questions may come with the right intentions—and while it is true that the Bible instructs you to read, meditate, and rightly divide the Word—they can often become judgmental or even accusatory. Questions like, *"How often do you read the Bible?"* could leave you feeling like you have fallen short. This mindset ties righteousness to actions, fostering a sense of lack:

"I'm not doing enough for God to be pleased with me."

These questions may unintentionally imply that your worth or relationship with God is dependent on how well you measure up to these practices. If you struggle to read daily or feel inadequate in your spiritual disciplines, these questions can foster guilt and condemnation rather than encouragement and growth.

But **everyone has a standard.**

Everyone has their own idea of what it means to be devoted to God. One person might ask, *"When was the last time you fasted?"* Another might say, *"When did you last lay hands on the sick?"* Then someone else might challenge them, *"When was the last time you visited the sick?"*

These questions often come from good intentions, but when we begin imposing our personal standards on others, we create an endless cycle of scrutiny. There will always be someone turning that same measure back on us. This is why works, in and of themselves, do not work. When we make righteousness about *doing* rather than *believing*, we turn grace into a burden instead of the gift it was meant to be. Grace lifts the weight that religious expectations place on people—it frees us to serve, not out of obligation, but out of love.

We may have a standard—but it is grace that not only teaches us about serving but also motivates and empowers us to do so.

Under grace, your actions are no longer driven by obligation but flow naturally from your relationship with God. Grace shifts the focus from outward effort to inward transformation. The Holy Spirit does not push or pressure. Instead, He leads and empowers you to live according to God's will through His love working within you. As you grow in Him, your desires begin to align with His, and the way you live is shaped not by external expectations, but by the vision He places in your heart.

When you understand this, the questions change. They are no longer focused on measuring your performance but on whether you are trusting the Holy Spirit to lead you and shape your walk with God. It is about responding to His love and *living out of the overflow* of what Christ has already accomplished within you.

Resting in Grace

Entering this rest means letting go of works-based righteousness and standing firm in God's grace. This kind of rest is not passive—it is a decision to fully rely on God's provision rather than your own strength.

The Sabbath Residing Within Us

The New Testament does **not** command observing the Sabbath as a specific day because Jesus fulfilled the law (**Matthew 5:17**). No, it does not mean stop attending church services. Gathering as believers is still important, but the point of this scripture is **not** about gathering—it is about *resting*. Our rest is now found in Christ, not in observing a specific day. This is where well-meaning believers can get trapped, thinking the focus is on attending a service rather than understanding the deeper reality of spiritual rest.

Paul affirms this in **Colossians 2:16-17**:
"Let no man therefore judge you in meat, or in drink, or in respect of a holyday, or of the new moon, or of the sabbath days: **Which are a shadow of things to come;** *but the body is of Christ."*

The Sabbath, like other Old Testament practices, was always meant to **point to Christ**. Now that He has come, the shadow is no longer needed because **the reality is found in Him**.

From Work to Rest

- **Freedom in Christ**: Salvation and righteousness come through faith, not through observing rituals (**Ephesians 2:8-9**).
- **True Rest in Jesus**: Jesus fulfills the Sabbath, offering daily spiritual rest and restoration.
- **Honoring God Beyond Traditions** – Believers can honor different traditions (going to church on Saturday or Sunday) while recognizing that true rest is found in Christ. Setting

aside time for worship is valuable, but genuine rest comes from trusting in Him.

Jesus invites us into this rest:
"Come unto me, all ye that labour and are heavy laden, and I will give you rest. Take my yoke upon you, and learn of me; for I am meek and lowly in heart: and ye shall find rest unto your souls. For my yoke is easy, and my burden is light" (**Matthew 11:28-30**).

True Sabbath rest is about living daily in the freedom and grace of God. It is not about striving but surrendering; not about doing but believing.

Conclusion

The Sabbath is no longer just a day—it is a **lifestyle** of resting in Christ. You are called to trust in His finished work, resisting the temptation to fall back into works-based righteousness. True rest is not found in rituals or specific observances, but in a relationship with Jesus. Think of it this way: If you had a wealthy benefactor who deposited an unlimited amount into your account, yet you kept working tirelessly to earn what was already freely given, you would be missing the gift. In the same way, Christ has already provided everything you need—peace, righteousness, and eternal rest. The only thing left is for you to receive it.

Jesus invites you into this rest, not just for a day, but for a lifetime:
"Come unto me, all ye that labour and are heavy laden, and I will give you rest..." (**Matthew 11:28-30**).

This is the invitation: a life where rest is no longer something you wait for—it is something you live in.

He calls you into this continual state of rest, where you walk in the joy and freedom of His grace. This is not a rest confined to a single moment, but an eternal invitation to trust in the One who is rest itself.

The Unshakable Promise of Grace

Salvation is not a fragile thing, and still some believers struggle with the fear of losing it. They wonder: What happens if I do not get everything right before Christ returns? What if I backslide? What if I fail too many times? These fears can feel overwhelming, but the truth of God's grace is unshakable.

The foundation of our salvation is not in our ability to hold onto God—but in God's ability to hold onto us. The Bible does not present salvation as something easily lost but as a firm, eternal promise secured by Jesus Himself.

When you fully understand this truth, you stop living in fear of failure and start walking in confidence, knowing that God's grace is stronger than your weaknesses.

God's Covenant of Unbreakable Grace

Throughout the Bible, God has always been a covenant-keeping God—He does not break His promises. The Old Testament is filled with shadows and types pointing to the eternal, unshakable nature of the New Covenant you now have in Christ.

Abraham's Covenant:
When God made a covenant with Abraham, it was not based on Abraham's ability to keep it. God alone passed through the sacrificial pieces (**Genesis 15:12-17**), signifying that the promise depended entirely on Him—not on Abraham's efforts.

David's Covenant:
God promised David that his kingdom would never end (**2 Samuel 7:16**). Even though David's descendants were unfaithful,

God's promise was not revoked. It was fulfilled in Jesus, the eternal King.

The New Covenant in Christ:

Jeremiah 31:31-34 foretold a better covenant, one where sins would be forgiven completely, and God's law would be written on our hearts. Jesus fulfilled this, securing our salvation once and for all.

God's pattern is clear: when He makes a covenant, He keeps it. If our salvation were dependent on our perfect performance, it would mean that we, not God, are the ones responsible for keeping the covenant. But Jesus sealed it with His blood (**Luke 22:20**), making it permanent, unshakable, and not based on our efforts.

Unconfessed Sin?

A common fear some believers have is: What if I sin and do not confess it before I die? But here is the truth—our salvation does not hinge on perfect confession.

Psalm 19:12 says:

"Who can understand his errors? Cleanse thou me from secret faults."

This verse acknowledges that we all have sins we do not even realize. If salvation required constant confession of every sin, no one could ever be saved! You literally would have to spend every waking moment asking for forgiveness. That is why Jesus' sacrifice covered all sin—past, present, and future (**Hebrews 10:14**).

If confessing every sin were required for salvation, that would put the burden back on us, making grace conditional instead of a gift. But the cross was a complete work.

Colossians 2:13-14 affirms this:

"And you, being dead in your sins... hath he

quickened together with him, having forgiven you all trespasses."

All trespasses—every single one—was forgiven at the cross. So, the question is not *"Have I confessed everything?"* but *"Do I trust fully in Christ's finished work?"*

What About Backsliding?

For many, the fear of backsliding is real. They worry that if they fall into sin, God will abandon them or that they will somehow lose their salvation—largely because this is what they have been taught. But the Bible paints a different picture, one that reveals God's grace and faithfulness even when we stumble.

First, let us define what backsliding means. Some assume it means losing salvation, but biblically, backsliding refers to turning away from God's ways, struggling with sin, or drifting in faith—not losing salvation altogether.

Hebrews 7:25 says:
"Wherefore he is able also to save them to the uttermost that come unto God by him, seeing he ever liveth to make intercession for them."

The phrase *'to the uttermost'* means completely and forever. If salvation could be lost, this verse would not be true. Backsliding does have consequences:

It weakens our fellowship with God—not our salvation, but our closeness to Him.

It can bring unnecessary struggles—just like a child who ignores their father's instructions may face hardship, a believer who drifts can experience spiritual difficulties.

It affects our peace and joy—David, after his sin, prayed: *"Restore unto me the joy of thy salvation"* (**Psalm 51:12**). He did not say, *"restore my salvation"*—because *he had not lost it.*

But here is the most important part: Even when we wander, God pursues us.

Luke 15:4 (The Parable of the Lost Sheep)
"What man of you, having an hundred sheep, if he lose one of them, doth not leave the ninety and nine in the wilderness, and go after that which is lost, until he find it?"

Jesus is not in the business of abandoning His sheep—He goes after them. He seeks, He restores, and He leads us back home. And that is the difference. Religion tells you that if you backslide, you have lost everything, and it is up to you to find your way back. But grace says, *"Even when you lose your way, I will find you."*

That is the heart of the Good Shepherd. That is the truth of the Gospel.

Those Who Fully Reject Christ

Some argue, *"What if someone completely turns their back on Jesus?"* Here is the hard truth—if someone walks away permanently, never repenting, never showing any fruit of salvation, the question is: Were they ever truly saved to begin with?

1 John 2:19 clarifies this:
"They went out from us, but they were not of us; for if they had been of us, they would no doubt have continued with us."

True salvation results in a transformed heart. If someone permanently rejects Christ, it reveals that they never had true saving faith.

But here is the difference: A struggling believer is different from an unbeliever. If you care about your faith, if you desire to follow God—even imperfectly—then that is proof that the Holy Spirit is at work in you.

Walking in Confidence, Not Fear

Salvation was never meant to be a guessing game. God wants us to be assured, not anxious.

Romans 8:1 gives us this confidence:
"There is therefore now no condemnation to them which are in Christ Jesus."

John 10:28 reinforces our security:
"And I give unto them eternal life; and they shall never perish, neither shall any man pluck them out of my hand."

When you put your faith in Christ, you are **sealed** with the Holy Spirit (**Ephesians 1:13**). That seal cannot be broken.

Does that mean you live recklessly? Of course not. But it does mean you live in freedom, not fear.

Final Thought: His Grace Holds You

If salvation were up to us, we would lose it every day. But thank God—it is not. You are saved by grace, not by works. Your salvation is not fragile—it is secure. Even in struggles, even in seasons of doubt, God remains faithful.

If you have ever worried about *'not getting it all right'* before Christ returns, take this to heart: He already did. (*Refer back to Chapter 17 and the scriptures found there*).

Dying to 'I': Seeing with Spiritual Vision

What is spiritual vision? What does it truly mean to see? This morning, as I spent time talking with the Holy Spirit, He revealed something profound: Masses of people live their entire lives trapped in a cycle, unaware of what they are in or how to rise above it. It takes spiritual vision to truly see.

For much of my life, my prayers were centered on requests like, *"God bless me," "Lord, let Your Spirit flow in this place,"* or *"Let revival come."* I prayed these with sincerity, not realizing that, according to the New Testament, these prayers had already been answered.

The Holy Spirit dwells within us. If He is inside me, then where was I asking Him to flow? If His Word declares that we are blessed, why was I still asking for blessings? Revival is not something we wait for—it is something already alive within us.

Spiritual Vision: A Shadow in the Old, Fulfilled in the New

Under the Old Covenant, people had to ask for their eyes to be opened to spiritual realities. A powerful example of this is found in **2 Kings 6:17:**

"And Elisha prayed, and said, Lord, I pray thee, open his eyes, that he may see. And the Lord opened the eyes of the young man; and he saw: and, behold, the mountain was full of horses and chariots of fire round about Elisha."

This moment occurred when the king of Syria sent an army to capture Elisha. His servant, seeing the enemy surrounding them, was filled with fear. But Elisha knew the truth—he was not alone. He prayed for his servant's eyes to be opened, and suddenly, the young man saw the heavenly army that had been there all along.

This passage illustrates how God's protection is always present, even when we do not see it. But it also reflects the difference between the Old and New Covenants. In the Old Testament, spiritual sight was something people had to ask for—something external, momentary, and dependent on a prophet's intercession.

Under the New Covenant of Grace, we already have spiritual sight through Christ. The Holy Spirit dwells within us, guiding us into all truth (**John 16:13**), and we no longer must ask for what has already been given—we simply need to renew our minds and walk in it. Your Spiritual Vision continues to sharpen more as you do this.

Paul speaks to this in **Ephesians 1:17-18**:

"That the God of our Lord Jesus Christ, the Father of glory, may give unto you the spirit of wisdom and revelation in the knowledge of him: The eyes of your understanding being enlightened; that ye may know what is the hope of his calling, and what the riches of the glory of his inheritance in the saints."

Through Christ, our spiritual eyes have been opened. Our role now is to align our minds with His truth. Instead of begging for sight, we meditate on His Word, allowing His wisdom to illuminate what is already within us.

This was a complete shift in my thinking. So often, people treat God as though He lives apart from us, as if He is external rather than dwelling within us. This mindset blinds you to the truth that you are already empowered with the Holy Spirit, fully equipped to walk in His promises. When you shift your perspective and see Him as the power within you, you begin to walk in true confidence and freedom.

Spiritual Vision: Seeing Beyond the Natural

Imagine a person who has lived in darkness their entire life. One day, a door opens, and light floods the room. At first, their eyes cannot handle it. The brightness is uncomfortable. Everything looks foreign, different, overwhelming. But as their vision adjusts, they realize they were never meant to live in darkness.

This is what spiritual vision does. It adjusts your sight so that you can see beyond natural circumstances, beyond religious traditions, beyond the limitations of the flesh. Spiritual blindness keeps people bound in cycles of defeat—stuck in the same patterns, praying for things that God has already provided, waiting for something to happen instead of stepping into what has already been given.

When Jesus healed blind Bartimaeus (**Mark 10:46-52**), something powerful happened.

- Bartimaeus threw aside his beggar's cloak—symbolizing that he was leaving behind his old way of living.
- He called out to Jesus—even when people told him to be quiet.
- And when Jesus asked, *"What do you want me to do for you?"* Bartimaeus did not say, *"Bless me."* He said, *"Lord, that I might receive my sight."*

You are not a beggar. You are fully provided for, spiritually and naturally by our Father. *"I have been young, and now am old; yet have I not seen the righteous forsaken, <u>nor his seed begging bread</u>."* **Psalms 37:25**.

Breaking Free from Religion

When you grow in vision, something uncomfortable happens—you start seeing things differently than others. This can be isolating at times.

For years, I poured myself into church activities—charity drives, skits, volunteering for anything and everything. I thought, *"This is what serving God looks like."* And while those things were good, I came to a moment when God pulled me in a different direction.

He was teaching me that service is not about religious activity—it is about obedience. I began hearing Him more clearly, but something happened—I felt resistance. When you no longer fit into the expectations others place on you, you may find yourself misunderstood or even rejected. But dying to 'I' means surrendering not only your plans—but also your need for approval.

Paul understood this struggle well. He said: *"For do I now persuade men, or God? Or do I seek to please men? For if I yet pleased men, I should not be the servant of Christ."* (**Galatians 1:10**)

If your focus is on pleasing people, you will always feel pressure to conform to what they expect. But when you live to please God, you walk in freedom.

When faced with offense, Jesus did not argue. He did not waste time debating those who refused to see. Instead, He kept moving forward in His purpose.

"A prophet is not without honour, but in his own country, and among his own kin, and in his own house." (**Mark 6:4**)

Not everyone will understand where God is taking you. And that is okay. Let go of the need to explain yourself. Visionaries are often misunderstood—until what God has spoken happens.

The Process of Spiritual Maturity

Growing in spiritual vision does not mean ignoring teachers, preachers, or biblical gatherings. These are vital. But scripture commands each of us to rightly divide the Word for ourselves. (**2 Timothy 2:15**)

As your vision sharpens, so does your ability to hear the Spirit more clearly. You begin discerning the difference between what sounds good and what is biblical. Conversations that once seemed normal start to sound *'off.'* You notice subtle deceptions of Satan that once went unnoticed. This is what it means to be spiritually awake.

But here is the key: Spiritual vision is useless unless you act on what you see.

Gifts or Fullness of the Spirit

Some believers operate in the **gifts of the Spirit** (**1 Corinthians 12**), such as prophecy, healing, wisdom, faith, and miracles, while others walk in the **fullness of the Spirit**. The Corinthian church, though spiritually gifted, was immature and often misused these gifts (**1 Corinthians 3:1-3; 1 Corinthians 14**).

Unlike the Corinthians, Jesus did not operate in spiritual gifts—He walked in **the fullness of the Spirit** (**John 3:34**). The gifts are pieces of the puzzle, but Jesus carried the full picture. The goal is to mature beyond occasional gifts and live daily in the fullness of His power. The more we die to self, the more we walk in that fullness.

Final Thought: Soar Like the Eagle

Do you recall the image of an eagle perched high on a rugged mountain cliff, overlooking a vast valley at the beginning? The wind rushes around it, but the eagle remains steady, its sharp eyes scanning the landscape. Unlike other creatures limited by what is directly in front of them, the eagle sees far beyond—spotting streams, prey, and hidden paths others cannot.

That is spiritual vision. The ability to rise above the noise, see clearly from a higher perspective, and recognize God's truth and direction, even when others only see obstacles. Dying to 'I' is the key to truly living in Christ. Let go of distractions. Let go of seeking approval. Step into the fullness of His Spirit. Because once you truly see—you can never go back.

The Most Intimate Relationship

For months, I found myself immersed in the Old Testament, reading account after account of God's people turning away from Him, experiencing the consequences, and yet continually being met by His mercy. At times, it was difficult to read—heavy with humanity's failures and the weight of sin. But then, amid those dark moments, glimpses of God's relentless faithfulness would emerge, and I would find myself feeling relieved: Whew!

I struggled with this—not because I did not understand it, but because my heart longed to run to the New Testament, to bask in the freedom of grace, the victory of Christ, and the power of His Spirit. I asked God, *"Why do You have me here?* Why not where my spirit feels lighter, freer?"

His response hit like lightning:

"Everything you read about Me—who I am, the miracles I perform—it is now in you. Every bit of who I am is in you."

I sat still, captivated. Every account of God's power, His authority, His mercy, and His miracles was not just a history lesson—it was a mirror, reflecting what He had placed within me. The same God who parted the Red Sea, shut the mouths of lions, and called fire from heaven now dwells inside me. And as a believer, He dwells in you, too.

That revelation stirred something inside me. It was not reading *about* what God had done—it was understanding this power alive within me. I was not just reading the Word—I was encountering the living God through it.

The Spirit Who Remembers

One morning, as I was reading the Old Testament, something wild happened—something that has happened several times.

I would be deep in scripture, lost in the moment, when suddenly, it was as if I were there—not just reading about it, but experiencing it. I could see the places, hear the voices, and feel the atmosphere. For a moment, it was like stepping into the pages of the Bible.

Then, it hit me.
That was not *my* memory.
That was the **Holy Spirit.**
He was there.
He remembers because **He witnessed it all.**

I had heard this idea mentioned in a sermon once—that the Holy Spirit remembers because He was there. But in that moment, it was no longer just something I had heard—it became real.

The Holy Spirit was there when the waters parted. He was there when Elijah called down fire. He was there when Jesus walked on water, when He broke the bread, when He hung on the cross and declared, *"It is finished."*

And now, **that same Spirit dwells in me.**

I sat there, overjoyed, and overwhelmed at the same time. The God of all eternity had placed His Spirit within me when I accepted Him—not just to teach me about Who He was, but to allow me to experience it. It was not just history anymore. It was not just words on a page. It was real. It was as if I was not just learning about God—I was being drawn into His story.

This is not just knowledge—it is communion. It is not just learning Scripture—it is hearing the voice of the One who wrote it. It is not just remembering history—it is stepping into the eternal.

More Than Just Learning—It Is Living

I have realized that the Holy Spirit is not just an observer or historian. He is the Revealer, the Teacher, the One who connects us to the very heartbeat of God. When He speaks, He does not just tell us about the past—He brings us into the eternal truth of it.

This is why Jesus said,

"But the Comforter, which is the Holy Ghost, whom the Father will send in my name, he shall teach you all things, and bring all things to your remembrance, whatsoever I have said unto you." (**John 14:26**)

This is why Scripture is alive. This is why God's Word pierces through time, space, and circumstance. Because it is not just words on a page—it is Spirit and life.

And this is the most intimate, fiery, unshakable relationship you will ever have.

I used to read my Bible just to gain knowledge. I would underline verses, memorize passages, and move on. But now, I pause.

I ask the Holy Spirit, *"What are You revealing?"*

I do not just read—I lean in. I do not just memorize—I watch, I wait, I listen.

Because walking with the Holy Spirit is not about collecting information—it is about stepping into revelation. It is hearing the very breath of God in the words He inspired.

This is the difference between knowing *about* God and knowing <u>Him</u>. This is the difference between reading scripture and experiencing the Author speaking it into your spirit. This is the difference between a ritual and a relationship.

More Today Than Yesterday

Romans 12:2 says:
"And be not conformed to this world: but be ye transformed by the renewing of your mind, that ye may prove what is that good, and acceptable, and perfect, will of God."

Transformation is not a one-time event—it unfolds daily. Each day is an invitation to see more, hear more, and walk bolder than before.

Imagine waking up with expectation:
"Lord, what will You reveal to me today? What truth will You unfold?"

This is not ritual—it is a living, breathing relationship. God is not calling you to simply read about Him; He is inviting you to step into the eternal.

Embrace His Presence

Through Him, scripture is no longer just a book—it is a conversation.

Through Him, you are not just learning about God—you are walking with Him.

Through Him, you are not just remembering the past—you are stepping into an eternal reality.

If you have ever longed for more of God, He has already given you every bit of Him.

If you have ever wondered where He is, He is within you.

If you have ever feared that you were missing something, then stop looking outward—start looking inward.

The Holy Spirit is not distant. He is not a mystery to chase—He is a Presence to embrace.

And when you live in that truth, nothing is impossible.

How It All Ties Together

After everything we have covered in this book, it all comes down to this: The wisdom of God is revealed by His Spirit. Without the Holy Spirit, the things of God seem like foolishness to the natural mind. But for those who are in Christ, you have been given access to the deep things of God.

Paul's words in **1 Corinthians 2** perfectly summarize everything this book has been about. It is not about human wisdom. It is not about man's ability. It is about Jesus, the power of the Holy Spirit, and the wisdom that comes only from God. This chapter is not about adding more teaching—it is about letting the Word speak for itself.

1 Corinthians 2

¹And I, brethren, when I came to you, came not with excellency of speech or of wisdom, declaring unto you the testimony of God.

²For I determined not to know any thing among you, save Jesus Christ, and him crucified.

³And I was with you in weakness, and in fear, and in much trembling.

⁴And my speech and my preaching was not with enticing words of man's wisdom, but in demonstration of the Spirit and of power:

⁵ That your faith should not stand in the wisdom of men, but in the power of God.

⁶ Howbeit we speak wisdom among them that are perfect: yet not the wisdom of this world, nor of the princes of this world, that come to nought:

⁷ But we speak the wisdom of God in a mystery, even the hidden wisdom, which God ordained before the world unto our glory:

⁸ Which none of the princes of this world knew: for had they known it, they would not have crucified the Lord of glory.

⁹ But as it is written, Eye hath not seen, nor ear heard, neither have entered into the heart of man, the things which God hath prepared for them that love him.

¹⁰ But God hath revealed them unto us by his Spirit: for the Spirit searcheth all things, yea, the deep things of God.

¹¹ For what man knoweth the things of a man, save the spirit of man which is in him? even so the things of God knoweth no man, but the Spirit of God.

¹² <u>Now</u> we have received, not the spirit of the world, but the spirit which is of God; that <u>we might know</u> the things that are freely given to us of God.

¹³ Which things also we speak, not in the words which man's wisdom teacheth, but which the Holy Ghost teacheth; **comparing spiritual things with spiritual.**

¹⁴ But the natural man receiveth not the things of the Spirit of God: for they are foolishness unto him: neither can he know them, because they are spiritually discerned.

¹⁵ But he that is spiritual judgeth all things, yet he himself is judged of no man.

¹⁶ For who hath known the mind of the Lord, that he may instruct him? **but we have the mind of Christ.**

Isaiah 55:8-9 says:
"For my thoughts are not your thoughts, neither are your ways my ways, saith the Lord. For as the heavens are higher than the earth, so are my ways higher than your ways, and my thoughts than your thoughts."

This seems to say that God's wisdom is far beyond human reach. Then, in **1 Corinthians 2:16**, Paul declares: *"For who hath known the mind of the Lord, that he may instruct him? <u>But we have the mind of Christ</u>."*

Do these two passages contradict each other? At first, it might seem that way. Isaiah emphasizes the vast gap between God's wisdom and human understanding, while Paul tells us that we have access to the very mind of Christ. But they work together.

Before Christ, humanity was limited—we could not grasp God's ways because we were spiritually dead. His thoughts were far beyond us, unreachable through human reasoning. But through Jesus and the Holy Spirit, that gap has been bridged. The mind of Christ does not mean we know everything God knows; it means we are led by His Spirit and can now understand the spiritual truths that were once hidden.

Yes, God's ways are still infinitely higher, but He has made His wisdom accessible to us through Christ. It is not about us trying to figure God out—it is about God revealing Himself to us. What was once a mystery is now an invitation into divine understanding, given freely through the Spirit.

This is it. This is everything!

The world cannot grasp it.
Religion cannot manufacture it.
Man cannot improve it.
And the enemy cannot stop it.

The deep things of God are revealed by His Spirit. And if you are in Christ, you have been given access to this wisdom, this power, this truth.

You have the mind of Christ.

This is how it all ties together.

And now, as you step into the closing chapter, let me share with you the most personal revelation God has given me—one that **changed everything...**

Be Still and KNOW That I AM GOD

For a long time, I was not sure how to end this book. Every morning, as I opened the Word, God would pour more into me—more about authority, more about grace, more about walking in His power. Each time I thought I had reached the conclusion, He revealed something deeper.

At one point, I even laughed and told my husband, *"I'm just gonna have to stop reading the Bible so I can finish this book!"* Because every time I opened the Word, God revealed something new.

I prayed, *Lord, at this rate, I will never finish!*

But now—I know.

I never quite felt satisfied—until the moment He spoke it.

A Dream That Changed It All

I woke up from another dream this morning. It was vivid—so real, so clear—that I could still feel it when I opened my eyes.

In the dream, my daughter and I were at a church gathering at my cousin's church in a nearby county. The room was full—mostly men, both young and old, but women were there too. The service was about to begin when I saw a person approach an older man in the room.

It was not anything out of the ordinary, just a simple interaction. The person whispered something, and immediately, the man responded with authority. He spoke directly to the issue—simply, with confidence, and without hesitation.

"It's gone. You're healed."

He smiled. That was it.

And the person walked away healed.

No one gasped. No one was shocked. Life continued as if this was the *'norm.'*

Because they expected it.

It was not some rare event— It was their reality.

Healing *was* expected. Miracles *were* expected.

And then—they worshiped.

But here is the part that hit me: they were not worshiping because of the healing.

Their praise had nothing to do with the miracle.

They worshiped simply because He is God.

It was not about what He had just done. It was about who He is.

It reminded me of **Luke 10:20**, when Jesus told the disciples:

"Rejoice not, that the spirits are subject unto you; but rather rejoice, because your names are written in heaven."

This is where I had missed it for so long.
My praises were mainly when I saw breakthrough, or a situation change. Of course, I praised Him other times, but it was still with lack of understanding. I used to feel joy when I saw a move of God and there is not anything wrong with praise.

But the people in my dream worshiped simply because their names were written in the Lamb's Book of Life.

And I sat there with tears just reverencing Who He was.

The Road and the Snakes

As the service was ending, we left, and as we got on the road, we encountered one of the largest snakes I had ever seen.

Its head was enormous, its mouth gaping open— disproportionate to the rest of its body.

As we passed it—it lunged at us.

My cousin and I were in the front seat of a convertible, with my children in the back. My son reached his hand out of the car.

I panicked.

"No! Get back in the car, son!"

But when I turned to my cousin—she was completely calm. She kept driving, completely unfazed.

We passed another snake—this one even stranger and just as large. Its mouth was lined with what looked like sheep's fur.

Again, I was alarmed.

"How do you endure all these snakes?" I asked.

She simply smiled as if that was normal.

We traveled further—and there was another one.

By now, I was thinking, *I just would not live here!*

But when we finally reached her home, the snakes were gone. It was as if they had never even existed.

Recognizing the Enemy

For years, as I have stated previously, snakes have appeared in my dreams, always representing an attack of the enemy. Every time I dreamed of snakes, I soon encountered distractions, challenges, or people Satan had deceived to be used against me.

But this dream was different. The snakes were not the focus. **My cousin's reaction was the lesson.** She did not acknowledge them. She did not swerve. She did not panic. She was not afraid. She just kept driving.

And when I woke up, God spoke immediately: *"Be still and know that I am God."*

Letting Go & Walking in Your Authority

Walking in authority is not just about fighting battles. Sometimes, it is about letting go. It is about resting in the finished work of Christ.

Again, **Romans 12:2** says: *"Be not conformed to this world: but be ye transformed by the renewing of your mind."* That means...

- If you feel hopeless—renew your mind to His Word.
- If your finances are in chaos—renew your mind to His Word.
- If your relationships are strained or others are coming against you—renew your mind to His Word.
- If your children have gone astray—renew your mind to His Word.

Become equipped. Know who you are in Christ so you can walk in your authority. For years, I begged God for help. I pleaded for prayers from others. I cried without realizing the authority inside me.

Do not let that be you.

Stop begging for what He has already given. Stop doubting what is finished. Seek God—but more importantly, seek to rightly divide His Word. Because when people begin to understand that the Old Testament was a shadow of the New and start reading scripture through the lens of grace, they are like the Israelites in **Ezekiel 36:12-14**, rising from the grave of spiritual deadness, stepping into the revelation of His truth—*Ye shall live!*

This is when you truly begin living your best life *in Him*. Verse 14 confirms that this revelation comes from the Lord Himself. And as you open your Bible, it is more than just reading—it is receiving revelation.

God is not exaggerating when He says He will open the windows of heaven. His Word is alive, powerful, and personal.

Even in details that seem obscure—the measurements in Ezekiel's vision, the long lists of genealogies (*begats*)—He speaks.

When you stop relying solely on someone else's interpretation and seek Him directly, your understanding deepens in ways you never expected.

His Word is power, and it will transform you.

The Greatest Cause for Rejoicing

At this point, you might still be processing everything you have read—reflecting on miracles, authority, and walking in revelation. But here is what matters most.

The miracles you see?

The breakthroughs?

The manifestations?

They are nothing compared to this one unshakable truth:

Your name is written in The Book.

That is everything. That is why you worship.

Not because of what He does. Not because of what He gives. Not because of what He changes.

You worship because of **Who He is**—and because **He is in you.**

I am saved.

If you have accepted Christ in your heart, you are saved. And currently, the Spirit of God is inside you, equipping you to walk in the authority He has already given.

So…

Be still.

Know.

He is God…because it changes – *everything*.

Thank You for Taking This Journey

I pray this book has encouraged, challenged, and strengthened you in your walk with Christ. If something you read spoke to your heart, helped bring clarity, or deepened your understanding of God's Word, I would love to hear about it.

Leaving a review is one of the best ways to help others discover this message. Your words could be the encouragement someone else needs to step into the fullness of what God has for them.

You can reach me at **letampatrick@gmail.com**—I welcome your thoughts, testimonies, and any way this book has impacted you.

Thank you for reading. My prayer is that you continue to grow, stand firm in truth, and walk boldly in the authority Christ has given you.

Blessings,

Leta M. Patrick

www.ingramcontent.com/pod-product-compliance
Lightning Source LLC
Chambersburg PA
CBHW020926090426
42736CB00010B/1050